Northumbria
TRUE TO THE LAND

The Hill Farming Photographs of Tony Hopkins

HALSGROVE

First published in Great Britain in 2003

Title page photograph: *The ploughing team waits at the gate; everything stops for a lost lamb. John Dodd and his daughter Frances Wise, Sillywrea Farm near Langley in south Northumberland.*

British Library Cataloguing-in-Publication Data
A CIP record for this title is available from the British Library

ISBN 1 84114 285 9

HALSGROVE

Halsgrove House
Lower Moor Way
Tiverton, Devon EX16 6SS
Tel: 01884 243242
Fax: 01884 243325
email: sales@halsgrove.com
website: www.halsgrove.com

Printed by D'Auria Industrie Grafiche Spa, Italy

Contents

Introduction   The Broken Token   5

 1 Speed the Plough   13

 2 Winter Fuel   19

 3 Three Ruins and Old Bones   31

 4 Working Woodland   41

 5 Traps and Tales   49

 6 Lucky Heather   63

 7 Catchy Weather   73

 8 Ditches and Dykes   85

 9 Summer Gather   93

10 Birkdale Clipping Day   107

11 Haying   119

12 Back End Sales and Shows   129

13 Sucklers   143

14 Kirn Supper   149

15 Deep Midwinter   155

Dosing Swaledale ewes in the pens on a wet April afternoon. Brian and Mary Bainbridge, Birkdale Farm in Teesdale, County Durham.

The Broken Token

A century or more ago in popular songs, when a labourer left the land and went to sea for seven years, he split a ring in two and gave half to his sweetheart. If he ever returned the broken token could be made whole again, to re-establish the bond.

I know very little about what it is like to be a farmer. Perhaps if I was from a farming background I would not see the drama and magic of it. Like most people, I am two or three generations removed from any direct contact with the land. My great-great-grandfather was a shepherd, my great-grandfather was a well-digger, my great uncle was a plough maker and my great-aunt was a farmer's wife. But any real connection with their countryside has been lost. This book holds out my half of the ring.

The photographs in the book are selected to follow particular themes that have interested me over the years: the way jobs are done, the humour and hardship of hill farming and rural industries, the inner workings of what has become a regional subculture. In the early 1990s, I was establishing a freelance career and winding down my job with a National Park Authority. Visiting farms and forests to take photographs was a way of celebrating the change – a sort of catharsis.

Most of the material for *True to the Land* was gathered in 1994 and 1995. I took two cameras out with me all the time, but concentrated on black-and-white photography. All the printing was done on the dining-room table, with half the house blacked out for a weekend at a time. This accounts for a distinct lack of professional polish in the prints, but at least I can claim it is all my own work.

Right from the start I knew the book's title and also some of the themes I wanted to explore. But the project was never finished. I had to make a living. Everything had to be shelved, quite literally, and it was only towards the end of 2002 that I took it down and started work on it again. It was tempting to add more photographs, more recent material or pictures that filled in some obvious gaps, but in the end I felt there would be more cohesion in it if I kept it as originally planned.

The text is new, benefiting from hindsight and making use of the breathless notes I took at the time.

Good pictures take themselves; some may be a disgrace from the technical point of view but they may still be honest and true to the moment. More than anything else I hope the photographs in this book tell stories about the link between people and the land, set in a contemporary context of traditional low-tech farming and associated industries.

The core material was gathered over a two- or three-year period. My collection of pictures reflected a time of continuity and gradual

Blackface tup in the judging pens at the Ingram Show. The white muzzle suggests there is a bit of Swaledale in his ancestry.

Top: *The Cheviot from Shill Moor. Late afternoon with the ice hardly melted and snow in the air.* Middle: *A breezy morning and bright sunshine. A Blackface ewe on the rim of Brough Law's Iron Age hill-fort in the Breamish Valley.* Bottom: *Haymaking at Ireshopeburn; the third day of sunshine.*

change, then of more rapid change. The Bainbridges of Birkdale retired, and with them passed the last family clipping day in Teesdale: Tom Foster the ploughman died; Molly the shepherd's cob was put out to grass. Then came BSE and the collapse of livestock values, supermarket strangleholds, foot and mouth disease and the scramble for stewardship grants.

Perhaps we really have reached a defining moment in the story of the uplands. The last generation born to the horse plough has retired, family farms are being sold and village pubs are catering for quiz nights and karaoke rather than dominoes and the accordion club. Whatever kind of land management lies ahead, even if protected landscapes embrace sustainable farming and can support local communities, a rift is opening between how things were on the land and how they will be.

Changing Ways

At one time or another each of England's northern uplands has been called the last wilderness. 'Wilderness' evokes images of a wide virgin landscape, untamed and unexplored, a distant land to people born in towns and cities. But the high hills and valleys of the Cheviots, the Wall Country and North Pennines have nothing in common with the Grand Canyon or the Masai Mara.

The modest landscapes of England, designated at their best as National Parks and AONBs, may have been shaped by the same raw elements as the great game or wilderness parks of the world, but they are too small and too useful to have been left to run wild. Every nook and cranny has been worked for thousands of years to grow crop and feed stock, to provide timber for beams and fences, to win stone and slate for walls and roofs and yield fuel for the hearth.

Over the centuries we have grown comfortable with our countryside; we have made an aesthetic and cultural virtue out of a necessity to exploit the land. It is only after visiting real wilderness areas around the world that the special qualities of our own countryside become apparent: the contract with nature: the accommodation and balance.

One of the threads running through the English countryside is that of constant change. Crops of corn may turn a field from green to gold in a matter of days, and a few months will see a generation of lambs born and sold. But these days politics and economics dictate that change in rural industries is quick and slick. Technology has come to the rescue of an expanding urban population; efficient food production has emptied the countryside of agricultural workers. Do we need to grow our own food at all?

Most of us live or work in towns and have only a distant understanding of how the land is exploited and managed. However, with only a couple of generations between us and our land-labouring ancestors our relationship with the countryside is complex, like that of a child to its parents or home, where any outward sign of change is for the worse. We may love the city for its fizz and sparkle, even its danger, but when we step out into fields we want to relax into security and substance.

Many writers today are quick to highlight the contradiction in our attitude to the countryside, making the point that working the land was never idyllic and that in the last few decades we have begun to look back with nostalgia to a time that never really existed. However, even in the sixteenth century when most of the population was still employed on feudal estates, Shakespeare was exploiting a sense of rustic innocence in *As You Like It*, where Corin the shepherd describes himself as:

> *…a true labourer. I earn what I eat, get that I wear; owe no man hate, envy no man's happiness; glad of other men's good, content with my harm; and the greatest of my pride is to see my ewes graze and my lambs suck.*

Shakespeare's words were intended to strike a chord with world-weary spivs, courtiers and merchants. Clearly, whether remembered or imagined, the loss of simple rural values was already deeply ingrained. Artists and visionary writers of the eighteenth and nineteenth centuries drew even more inspiration from the countryside, not merely as a neutral background to their painting or writing, but as a context for it. Reynolds made a living by painting rich patrons' wives dressed in shepherds' clothes; Gainsborough and Constable both had a passion for landscape and the working countryside; John Clare was born into rural poverty and survived by selling charming verse; Samuel Palmer caught his Valley of Vision in a few ink sketches; Ruskin and Morris agonised for years over the social fabric of the land. All of them saw in their mind's eye a landscape that lived and breathed, full of birds and butterflies and people. None of them foresaw tractors, let alone genetically modified crops.

Most Victorian landscape painters avoided real people. Radical estate-owners had created an organised landscape, the fields bursting with efficient new crops and stock breeds; farms were model villages, cottages were dressed to be picturesque.

Into this spotless scenery were painted cheerful swains and milkmaids, with clean hands and rosy cheeks, content with their modest lot. The threat of civil unrest meant that the ruling classes of the day were uneasy with pictures of grim-faced labourers. Scenes of harvest-home were a fiddle-tune away from scythe-wielding mobs burning haystacks as a prelude to revolution. Working figures in farmscapes receded to coloured dots.

Yet despite the hardship there was no revolution, and by the turn of the century most of the population had moved away from the land and were working in factories. Of course, there was still a link with what had been left behind, and with a general improvements in living standards for those still involved in rural industries, the whole country began to bask in an Arcadian glow; the nation was at last united with its rural heritage, at a safe distance, and from this emerged the Women's Institute, *Lark Rise*, Elgar and sliced bread. It is perhaps no coincidence that this was also the time for photography to make a genuine bid to capture the humanity of work on the land, rather than to feed a stereotype and strike a fashionable pose.

Before the Fall

The Great War changed things again, in every corner of the land: not just in a practical way, but in the minds of everyone who had waved ploughboys and shepherds away to the Somme – in the perception of lost innocence. Work on the land carried on as it had before, at a steady pace and in familiar fields. The shortage of manpower encouraged mechanisation, and in time this would have transformed rural industries, but of course, another war intervened.

Thus the 1940s and '50s witnessed the fading of horse power and the rapid rise of the tractor, the drive to increase productivity and a shake-up for the thousands of small-scale businesses that supported and served rural communities. In recent years, with the demise of family farms and social infrastructure, and the advent of hobby-farming and the 4x4, it has become fashionable and convenient to reflect wistfully on better times 'before the Fall', before the Great War, before the countryside needed to be managed.

Now, when we see a photograph of someone at work in a field, with feet firmly in the earth, we cast our minds back down the years. It must, we think, have been long ago. We root about in antique shops among piles of old postcards and prints, pulling out creased, blurred snapshot of Land Girls hoeing turnips, then searching the faces half expecting to recognise our great-aunts and grandmothers. And when we peer at faded sepia school portraits and pictures of picnics at haymaking time, we are looking for ourselves.

I believe in the spirit of the land. Not in every handful of earth or each leaf as life from eternal life, but in what the countryside means to each of us and how we respond to it.

The best kind of art involves the emotions. I don't know if it would have been possible to have taken these photographs fifty years ago, before SLR cameras and fast film. Most of the best twentieth-century 'working countryside' pictures I have seen – those carrying an emotional charge – have been paintings, by Becker, Soper, or Tunnicliffe.

What I tried to do when I took my camera into the farmyards of Northumbria was to faithfully 'see' what was there and to be honest about it, in the same way that these artists, illustrious or obscure, were honest. Not the contrived world of Frank Sutcliffe, but the mud-and-bullets world of Robert Capa. The art could take care of itself.

This then is a book about the land as it is or was a moment ago, seen through the day-to-day work of those still in touch with its essential values. None of the photographs is deliberately staged, nobody asked for payment and nothing has been included that cannot still be found somewhere in the Northumbrian hills. But only just.

Checking the ewes at lambing time. Michael and Richie Jameson with quad bike and dog, looking west towards Queen's Crag, West Hotbank Farm, north of Hadrian's Wall.

Three generations of gamekeepers burning heather on an April morning: Richard, Denis and Bill Smailes of Harehope in north Northumberland.

Three generations of wallers: George, Thomas and Tom Hall of Coquetdale in mid-Northumberland. Halfway along a stretch of drystone wall at Park Hall Farm.

Exercising pigeons at a creel on old mine workings at Cockfield Fell, County Durham. Miners have always appreciated freedom, living it vicariously through animals and birds.

Retired miner Million Makepeace with one of his favourite pigeons, at Butterknowle, County Durham.

John Reading, pig manager at New Bewick, north Northumberland. Not all countryside jobs are fun all the time.

John Dodd ploughing Second Low Field, Sillywrea Farm, Langley in south Northumberland, where the North Pennines meet the Tyne Valley. John still uses Clydesdales for most farm work: 'If I didn't have the horses I might not have any arable, just grass, and buy what grain and straw I needed. More grass would mean I keep more livestock, but I wouldn't make any more money; any extra from the livestock would go on buying foodstuff. But I like to keep tillage, to grow what we need and keep the horses working.'

ONE

Speed the Plough

The 'Vision of Piers Plowman' was written by William Langland around 1380. In it, a weary traveller dreams he is in a wilderness among a crowd. He is told by a mysterious fair lady that everyone there is seeking worldly success, but that there are more important spiritual values to strive for. Eventually everyone is convinced that they should search for Truth but nobody knows how. They turn to a ploughman, Peter, who agrees to guide them:

> I wol worshipe therwith Truthe by my lyve,
> And ben His pilgrym atte plow for povere mennes sake.
> My plowpote shal be my pikstaf, and picche atwo the rotes,
> And helpe my cultour to kerve and clense the futwes.

(I will devote my life to the worship of truth, I will be his pilgrim, following the plough for the sake of poor people. My plough-shoe will be my pikestaff, to cut through the roots and help my coulter to turn the furrows.)

After a series of adventures and disappointments – lasting hundreds of pages – during which the crowd turn against the ploughman and the traveller despairs of finding 'Truth', he is set back on his way by 'Conscience'. After this he dedicates himself to becoming a pilgrim and seeking out and following the ploughman. Of all things in the world, it is the honesty of the plough that leads to Truth.

Lane Foot Lea

I followed John Dodd and his horses many times in the mid-1990s. A true 'Pilgrym atte plow', his farm near Langley is probably the last in the country to rely on horse power for day-by-day duties: carting muck, cutting hay, sowing corn. But it is the ploughing that is most magical. It all looks so effortless, timeless, essential. I had recently seen Bronze Age plough-marks beneath the turf of the Cheviots and was especially keen to be at Sillywrea Farm when John next ploughed a grass field – a piece of fresh ground.

The lea or sown pasture of the Lane Foot had stood for six years as fallow in a rotation – two or three crops of barley, then a crop of turnips, then another two of barley, then down to grass. This was the fourth time the lea had been ploughed out. Knowing where to begin was the hardest part.

I could see no break in the cropped sward but to John's eye there was a clear ridge where the previous start had been made. Short white-

Ploughing stubble on the Thackey Field, Sillywrea Farm. John Dodd with his favourite Ransome horse plough. The field is very stony and John stopped a couple of times to dig out boulders. 'We'll not get the benefit, but others will.'

topped sticks were set out at either end of each break or section, then a marking furrow was taken out all around the edge of the field, 4½ yards from the wall to leave a big enough headland for the plough to turn. The first furrow, carefully lined up and 30 yards from the left edge, set the first break into place.

'Measure 30 yards from the edge of the ploughing; that leaves 20 yards' fellying, then you'll gather another 20 yards and that leaves you with 20 yards in the middle between the two gatherings.' A gathering is where the plough works wider and wider, a fellying where it narrows. Because single-furrow ploughs can only work in one direction, casting to the right, a system has to be followed to make sure there are no gaps. A pattern of rectangles soon appears out of the confusion.

Three elements work together to make ploughing easy: the plough, the team of horses and the man driving. The plough, at least, has no mind of its own. At its simplest it has a coulter to mark a vertical line, a share to cut a horizontal slice, and a mould-board to twist the slice over against the previous row.

But to achieve this, and to have it glide straight and true, needs fine adjustment. First the buck or bridle has a half-moon of notches which can be reset if a horse is pulling keen, then there is another row of notches at the front so the chain can be raised to pull the point down, and the sheath or bar running the length of the plough can be altered at the back to set the point up. The furrow-wheel is fixed according to how wide the furrow should be, narrower for grass than for stubble, and the coulter can be angled to keep it tight against the

Dancers blacked-up for Border Morris at Bowes Museum near Barnard Castle, County Durham.

furrow. Most important of all, the coulter-blade can be moved forward or backward from the plough point. An inch or two makes a big difference.

For most work John sets the Ransome plough level, or with a slight tilt away from the furrow to make the cut slightly deeper on the land side, and has the coulter about two inches from the body of the plough. With everything in order and the horses steady it should be possible to let go of the stilts and step out of the furrow. It is a matter of the ploughman guiding rather than wrestling with the plough.

John talked to his horses:

> 'H'ad-up! H'ad-up!
> 'Steady now, steady; not in o'er big a rush.
> 'Tch, tch... J'up!
> 'H'away man, Monty!'

With short days, the Lane Foot would take more than a week to finish, at a good pace and without a stop for rain. Towards the end of the morning John looked across the valley to Lough Green Farm where his neighbour had been out in a tractor with a four-row plough. The field had taken him about five hours; the tractor cost over £30,000.

Tom Foster

Tom was eighty-eight when I first met him and he had been ploughing since he was eight. At first he had followed his father from farm to farm in Tynedale, taking on work at Hexham Hiring Fair. By the age of nineteen he was head horseman and loved the life.

A day's work started at 5am with a cup of tea and a walk to the farm. At 6am the horses were fed and groomed to be taken out at 7am. Breakfast for the labourer/ploughman was home-cured ham and egg, taken in the field at about 8.30am. At midday the horses were led back for a rest; afternoon work started at 1pm, with the women of the farm bringing out tea at about 4pm. The day finished at 6pm, often later. At 8pm the horses had to be groomed and fed and the ploughman then had to walk home for a supper of a ham sandwich and a glass of milk.

It sounded a gruelling existence to me, but as he described it, seventy years on, Tom was reliving a time of sunshine and milkmaids, of stopping the horses to lift lapwing nests out of the way, and listening for corncrakes and cuckoos on summer mornings.

From 1940, Tom had worked on the Wallington estate, with tractors. When he retired from farm work in 1971, he continued as a freelance ploughman, with his own tractor and four-row plough. I photographed him at Beaumont House Farm where he was at work on a field of set-aside rape, preparing it for a wheat crop. He had ploughed the same field in 1921.

I called to see him several times when I was passing Wallington, most recently in the spring of 1995. He lived alone, a widower with no family, in a little L-shaped room next to the clock tower of Wallington Hall. My notebook reads:

Tom heavy-boned, stooped. Weathered face and grey eyes. Big hands. Rather deaf and with a burr to his voice. Wearing a threadbare boiler-suit with a big hole in the elbow. The room bare – nothing on the walls. Tom sitting close to the fire, in a rocking chair with an old sack as cushion-cover. Coal ash over the mat and hearth. On the mantelpiece his pipe and tobacco pouch and a jar of marmalade. Talked about times long past. His tractor outside has a leaking sump but he is still looking for work at nearly ninety.

He died at ninety-one, a year after he could plough no more.

Gradely Lasses: a dance team from Pontefract, dancing to 'Speed the Plough' at the Teesdale Thrash at Bowes Museum.

Tom Foster adjusting his four-furrow reversible plough at West Pasture, Beaumont House Farm. Tom first ploughed this 15-acre field in 1921 and it would have taken him a fortnight, using a team of horses. On this day in September 1994, it took about five hours.

Tom Foster's favourite photograph of himself – he liked it because it showed off the furrows. The last crop in this field had been oilseed rape: 'There's millions of slugs after the rape is cut. Plough them eight inches deep and you'll fettle 'em.'

Tom Foster, probably the oldest working ploughman in England when I took this photograph at Beaumont House Farm in 1994. He was eighty-eight and still looking for work. 'If I was to give up I'd just sit around, man. I'd just die.' The farmer at Beaumont House knew Tom would make a perfect job of the field but was worried about him and his tractor on the open road.

Maggie Dodd letting out the hens at Harlow Field.

TWO

Winter Fuel

On cold winter evenings I light a fire in the living room. This creates havoc with the thermostat and the central heating turns itself off so that the rest of the house is freezing by bedtime. But there is something very satisfying about a real fire: a direct link with the elements and the simple imperative of keeping warm.

Wood, peat and coal are the free fuels of the northern hills. In their time, each has served as a day-to-day necessity. I was brought up huddling around a smouldering coal fire and the romance of it wore thin, as it must have for many a shivering ploughboy or serving maid.

At one time there were little bell pits or family drift mines all the way from Cockfield Fell to the Kyloe Hills and people gathered sea coal from the beaches. These days most farm hearths still burn coal, augmenting cental heating of one sort or another, but the coal comes from deep mines a thousand miles away. I tried bringing back sea-coal from the beach at Lynemouth once, but burning it was like trying to warm yourself on whin boulders: no heat or flame, and a lot of sulphureous fumes. No romance; no wonder people prefer to spend money on good quality coking coal. Peat, on the other hand, is a joy and it is surprising that few shepherds still exercise their right to cut at least a little.

Peat develops in thick beds where the ground is cold and waterlogged. It is abundant on the acid hilltops and blanket bogs of northern England but has become scarce in the lowlands because of drainage and large-scale exploitation for garden compost. There is a conservation issue about any peat digging these days, but in the uplands it is hard to see how modest domestic use could ever have done very much harm.

My first proper introduction to peat digging came when I visited Lewis in the Outer Hebrides. It was July and everyone seemed to be out cutting and stacking peats. I spent an afternoon at Coig Peighinnean in the company of a crofter who plied me with several glasses of whisky and four sacks of peat, which I brought home for us to use on special occasions like New Year's Eve. The earthy smell of burning peat goes very well with 'Auld Lang Syne' and a glass of Talisker.

A few times, especially when walking over the Pennine moors, I have seen stacks or rickles of peat drying in summer sunshine miles from the nearest farmhouse. More often I have noticed grassed-over workings, long deserted.

When I took Willie Taylor up the College Valley in the Cheviots to see the steep barren slopes he once shepherded, he pointed out the peat beds high above Coldburn where he had used a horse sled to lead the peats down to the cottage. It looked as if it must have been hard work and it was no surprise that, as far as Willie knew, nobody in the College Valley still bothered.

But I discovered that two of the Coquetdale shepherds did, and the following summer I called several times to see John Short of Carlcroft, who worked a bed up on Gowky Shank. He had first cut peats when he was eight and had been at Carlcroft for twenty-five years. In his early days all the 'top-end' families had relied on peat for their fuel, cutting a year's supply with a year in hand, 80 cart-loads from hill to house and all the neighbours helping.

I walked up the steep path of White Rigg to see the cutting in progress that June and to see the rickles being stacked and sorted and finally led in. Days of heavy labour, but John was lyrical about it: 'An evening in August I'll be by here looking the sheep and I'll mebbe stop and rerickle the peats. You can't beat it man; you're just working for yourself.'

Burning Logs

Gathering your own fuel can be as satisfying as catching or growing your own food. It can also be as desperate a challenge. In the 1990s I watched television images of Rwandan refugees scavenging like ants on the Zambian border for anything they could cook or burn, leaving a wasteland where there had been a forest. Then in Bosnia the news bulletin showed families sitting at their only meal of the day, pumpkin pie, steamed over a fire of tree roots dug from what had been field hedges. All the proper wood had been used up the previous summer: anything burnable had vanished from the land. The replacement field

Fox tracks along a snowy path through mixed woodland with beds of woodrush. South Tyne Valley near Haydon Bridge.

John Short sharpening the cutting blade on the flouter.

With the top 6 inches of turf removed the peats can be cut, using a winged peat spade. Bob is forking out the peats, still waterlogged and heavy, for Kieran to lay them in a herring-bone pattern to part-dry them in the sun.

Tools of the trade: gripe, peat knife, peat spade, flouter, ritting spade and fork. Bob Black and Kieran Howley (students at Kirkley Hall Agricultural College) with John Short, shepherd at Carlcroft in Coquetdale in the Cheviot Hills, Northumberland.

Late June on Gowky Shank. After a few weeks a dry skin forms on the peats and they repel water. John Short is building a 'rickle' or peat stack, 5 feet high and on a pallet so the bottom peats are not spoilt. The rickle is igloo-shaped at the base and beehived at the top, allowing the breeze to work through the whole stack.

Rickles on White Rigg. In the vastness of the Cheviot massif the peat stacks resemble a megalithic monument or stone circle. White Rigg probably gets its name from the cotton-grass blanketing the wet ground. This stretch of the Border Ridge is Carlcroft's traditional peat-gathering area; these rickles will provide half of John Short's fuel for the coming winter.

The skeletal remains of Blawearie on Bewick Moor in north Northumberland. The farmhouse has been derelict for over fifty years but is it still the only shelter for miles around. Dead bracken clothes the slopes now but a century ago it would have been harvested as bedding.

THREE

Three Ruins and Old Bones

Deserted dwellings often have an eerie atmosphere, especially when they are in remote places. In towns and villages, old houses are demolished or renovated, but in the hills they are often left to rot.

When I knew I was moving to Northumberland in 1980, I had copies of the *Hexham Courant* sent to me so that we could look for a cottage somewhere a few miles from town, preferably in the country. What I did not realise was that there was no such thing as a cottage in the country, that in the real world there were just cold damp barns in the middle of nowhere, with no facilities or services. We reviewed our options and moved into Hexham, round the corner from the local school and the pub.

While walking along forgotten hill paths, I have often come across the stone quoins and footings of sheilings, dating back to medieval times when cattle were summered on the hills and herders lived in temporary dwellings. Wolves and reivers were a constant threat and according to respectable travellers the land yielded 'nothing but mysery'.

Later in the Border Wars, most ordinary people built their homes of wood and got used to seeing them burnt down; little has survived. The more affluent farmers and clerics of the sixteenth century lived in fortified bastles and peles with 5-foot-thick walls; many of these austere buildings still exist in one form or another, often as barns but rarely as comfortable homes.

It was only in the eighteenth and early-nineteenth centuries, in more peaceful times, that family farmhouses appeared and the wastes were reclaimed for pasture. Times were never easy and raising a family must have been downright hard but I imagine most children who grew up on lonely farms had fond memories of sunny days and skylarks. In the end most sons and daughters had to leave to find a living elsewhere, on better land, in factories and in service.

Burn Divot and Blawearie

North of Hadrian's Wall, close to where it was breached in the Barbarian Conspiracy of 367AD, over the Tipalt Burn and along a windswept track, through a prairie of purple moor-grass, miles from a road and out of sight of any other farm or dwelling, is the ruin of Burn Divot.

I found it one early-autumn morning when I was looking for a view of the Border mires and saw the low stone walls on the skyline of a 'cuesta' ridge. Close up, it was clear that Burn Divot had been built to a typical laithe-house design with a single line of buildings including byre and farmhouse. The roof had gone completely but there was still a rusty range in the kitchen. The windows were all square with heavy stone sills and lintels and no frames.

After wandering in and out of the rooms, it was the house's lidless eyes that held my attention. Each had its own staring view of stark emptiness, a landscape of horizontal streaks washed isabelline and orange by drifts of cotton-grass. It was treacherous country, bogs all the way to Moss Peteral and the Whin Sill. To live here people must have been self-contained and calm. On this blustery bright day you could pick out patches of sphagnum moss and a shallow ridge marking a secret way travelled by generations of rustlers and thieves. I don't think I would ever have felt comfortable at Burn Divot. I would have spent my days and nights at the windows looking to see who or what was coming to call.

Not all ruins are quite so creepy. In the middle of Bewick Moor near Alnwick there is a steading rejoicing in the name of Blawearie. Again it is miles from anywhere, on a great plateau of high heather caught between bitter easterlies and damp westerlies; there is always a wind on Bewick Moor.

Dramatic and derelict for fifty years, Blawearie is well-known to local walkers and is a perfect place for a picnic. People speak in fond terms of its sheltered setting, tucked in against a sandstone outcrop with green paddocks and what must once have been a secret garden. Nobody thinks there are ghosts about, even though it is only a hundred yards from a Bronze Age burial cairn and the moor is littered with prehistoric earthworks and rock art.

The first time I explored Blawearie's nettle-filled rooms in 1982 it still had a roof and the byre was full of straw. It all looked so idyllic that it was hard to understand why anyone would have wanted to leave, whatever the isolation. In fact it transpired that the last tenants had been the Army, who had taken over the moor as a practice range in the early 1940s.

Before that the Rogerson family had lived here – a large happy family if their faded photographs are anything to go by. Rogerson was shepherd to the Harehope Estate and in those days, as in medieval times, you lived close to your flock. Alas, Blawearie's roof and its gable end are gone – deliberately demolished – and people say the atmosphere just isn't the same. The last time I was there, the ruin had lost its ramshackle charm but the setting was still glorious and the wind still blew.

Roofs are taken for granted unless something goes wrong with them. In Northumbria the traditional material is usually sandstone, cut thin and shaped to size, with the smallest flags run along the top of a roof and the biggest ones along the bottom. Most of the weight is carried by the middle timbers. It is only when you get close that you realise how massive old roofs are and how heavy they must be.

When Matthew Charltons were replacing the laths and rafters of the fourteenth-century pele tower at Elsdon in Northumberland I had the chance to see the work in progress, climbing the tower steps and edging around the scaffolding to watch the old flagstones

Old sheep bones and wooden pegs, used to hold the stone slates in place on the roof of the vicar's pele, Elsdon in Northumberland.

being set back in place. These great stones probably graced the original roof and survived the fires of the Scottish Wars in an inhospitable climate.

A rector who lived here for three years wrote that he had to sleep 'in the parlour, between two beds, to keep me from being frozen to death, for as we keep open house, the wind enters from every quarter, and are apt to creep into bed with one.' Clearly the thick walls and solid roof failed to keep the weather out.

Close up the roof flags looked immense, hard to manipulate and brutal even to calloused hands. The original pegs to hold the flags in place on the laths were sheep bones; these were being reused even though they would be invisible from the outside. It was an impressive and authentic enterprise: the whole roof fixed in place by a few old bones. Bracing myself against the west wind I watched for half an hour but the tower seemed far more precarious from above than below and I was glad to come down.

Good roofing stone is hard to come by these days, which explains why so many old barns are stripped to their skeletal rafters. Every village and almost every farm once had its own quarry for walling stone. Finding evenly-bedded sandstone for specialist purposes was more difficult. Welsh slate and cheaper composite materials are now available everywhere, which means that one roof looks like any other. But if like me you live in an old house your attitude to slates is probably practical rather than picturesque.

Stone Slate and Black–thack

The little quarry of Ladycross, near Slaley on the edge of the North Pennine moors, is an example of how top-quality stone is still won and worked. The quarry has been open for about three centuries and all the roofs of nearby Blanchland are witness to the durability of its sandstone. Only a few years' supply of quality stone is left.

When I was last there one of the workmen was walking ahead of the mechanical shovel, collecting frogs in a bucket so they would not be squashed. Ladycross is a hand-worked quarry and the whole workforce (eight at the time – it is now just four) takes a pride in the wildlife that occurs there.

The manager, Colin Jewitt, is a down-to-earth visionary and an excellent naturalist: for at least twenty years he has been creating ponds and meadows on the site so that when it closes as a quarry it will have a new lease of life as a nature reserve. He pointed out palmate newts in the puddles and crossbills in the pines and we spent some time talking about the best meadow flowers to attract bumble-bees. Meanwhile the noise from heavy hammers and a circular saw echoed around the rock faces and dust settled into my hair and onto the camera lens.

The last of my trio of isolated ruins looked at first sight to be in at least as bad a state as Burn Divot and Blawearie. Levy Pool lies in a fold of rushy pasture on Cotherstone Moor, above Bowes in County Durham.

I saw it for the first time when I was researching the *National Trail Guide to the Pennine Way* in 1988. Having walked north from the pretty village of Bowes, I found myself on a dead-end road through fenced MoD land with fading notices warning me of poison gas. After a mile the road ended and there was a wet field full of lapwings and redshanks. A path veered right, into the valley of the Deepdale Beck, and there was Levy Pool, a crumbling farmhouse sheltered by a stand of tall sycamores.

It had no roof and the main gable was half-fallen, but what caught my eye was the byre, which had a black roof-topping of what I knew must be heather. 'Black-thack' had been a traditional roofing material long before stone and slate, but from what I could remember there were only a handful of examples left in England. It was a big surprise to find one here. I explored the ruins and found a datemark of 1776 above the farmhouse door. It was obvious from the steep pitch of the roof that the farmhouse had been thatched, as well as the outbuildings, but nothing now remained.

In the byre I had a careful look at the roof and found it was made up of bolted A-frames and sawn purlins; the rafters were untrimmed pine stems, nailed to the ridge and supported at the eaves. The mouse-infested layer of heather was a foot thick and ready to disintegrate.

I continued my walk north over Cotherstone Moor to Lunedale wondering if I could find out anything about Levy Pool from County Council contacts. 'Knowing how way leads on to way'. I doubted if I would ever return, but I did. I discovered a few months later that the place had been sold and someone was applying for grants to do building work. I wrote the first edition of the Pennine Way guide assuming that by the time it was published Levy Pool would be unrecognisable.

I contacted the Beamish Museum who had a photograph of the farm around 1916, when it was occupied by the Addison (or Robinson?) family. The photograph showed the main line of buildings thatched. The sycamores were only as high as the farmhouse chimney, while in the background on the skyline there was a pine wood. In the book I set this photograph next to a recent one and suggested walkers on the Pennine Way might like to take their own for comparison.

One of the interesting points from this exercise was that over the century the sycamores have grown while the pine wood has disappeared. The pine and the heather must have been immediately to hand when Levy Pool was built but the world had changed around it. The land had been bought by the MoD who had used it as a firing range. Apparently, the pines died and when they were cut down they were found to be full of shrapnel.

Whilst revising the Pennine Way book for a new edition in the 1990s, I made a detour, not strictly necessary, up the road from Bowes. The barbed wire and poison-gas notices were still there. So were the lapwings.

I did not know what to expect when I took the path down to Deepdale, but against all the odds there was Levy Pool, intact and with its gable end restored. Not only that but there were big piles of fresh heather at the gate waiting for thatchers to arrive from York. I called in and spoke to the owner, a masonry contractor, and discovered he was having the farmhouse rethatched and although the byre roof was to be dismantled it seemed to me that the spirit of the place had survived. Levy Pool had cheated death and held on to its hat.

Roofing work on Elsdon Pele. This is the first time the roof has been repaired on this medieval 'fortified parsonage' for at least a century; it must have been a perilous work-place without the benefit of scaffolding.

Putting back the stone slates after replacing the laths on the roof of Elsdon Pele. A strong north-westerly breeze is billowing the red flag on the tower's chimney.

Barrowing bundles of heather for the roof of Levy Pool farmhouse, near Bowes in County Durham. The steeply-pitched roof of the farmhouse has been rebuilt and is three-quarters rethatched in traditional 'black-thack'. When it was last thatched the heather would have been gathered within sight, off Cotherstone Moor, but this time it has been bought in from Kirkbymoorside. Mid-June, but the ash is hardly into leaf and the sycamore is battling against a cold wind. Lapwings and curlews, with fledged young, call all the time from the pastures.

William Tegetmeier (carrying the bundle) and Aron Greenwood thatching the roof of Levy Pool farmhouse. The rafters are covered with a layer of turf before the thatch is added. Half the work for a thatcher is done on the ground, getting things ready. It will take about seven weeks for the two men to finish the job. The byre roof on the right is not being rethatched and has since been dismantled.

William Tegetmeier of York on the roof of Levy Pool Farm, near Bowes, County Durham. William is an experienced thatcher with straw, but very few people these days get the chance to work with heather. The only other 'black-thack' building I know is at Causey House near Vindolanda. The main change in heather-thatching technique over the centuries is that the bundles of heather, laid upside down and horizontally across the turf layer, are now fixed in place by metal rods and hooks.

Above: *Ladycross Quarry near Slaley, close to the Northumberland/Durham border. The thin horizontal beds of carboniferous sandstone produce attractive roofing slates as well as lintels, paving flags and cladding. In the background, behind the bed of sandstone where John Davidson is working, is the 'over-burden' of clay with coal seams.*

John Davidson using a mash-hammer and bolster to cut stone slates at Ladycross Quarry.

Stonework is often a matter of brute force and a big hammer: Bob Green, then foreman of Ladycross Quarry, using a 28lb mell-hammer to break down a thick bed of sandstone for rockery stone.

Davy Milburn using a comb-chisel to cut out a bird-bath, Ladycross Quarry.

By the time timber is ready to harvest no one can remember what it was planted for. Small-scale extraction is relatively costly and therefore not very profitable. Jonathan Beniams is felling a spruce tree in a 2-acre plantation near Sewingshields, having taken on the job of thinning three woods and clear-felling another; twelve week's work extracting 700 tons of timber. 'Those were some cold days there,' said Johnny afterwards. The small-wood went to Eggers for chipboard; the main stems or logs went for milling, to be made into pallets and posts.

FOUR

Working Woodland

The only really extensive forests in Northumbria are plantations of Sitka spruce, often in monoculture but sometimes with ribbons of the original mixed oak woods on the margins or along watercourses. Less broadleaved woodland survives in the North East than in any other region of England. In County Durham the prettiest fragments are in clefts of the magnesian limestone, like Castle Eden Dene, which were too steep to clear or to replant and are now nature reserves.

In between the coastal valleys and towards the Pennine moors most of the landscape is a lattice of open fields and ex-mining villages and there are some treeless settlements with inappropriate names like Evenwood and Woodland. But over the next brow there is Hamsterley with its extensive managed forest, and you realise that there is still somewhere for the squirrels to go, even if they have to make do with alien conifers.

The Forestry Commission planted some huge blocks of conifers on the 'marginal' land of northern England in the postwar years, when the agency was charged with the simple task of growing trees. For half a century nobody seriously questioned the quality of the woodland that was being produced, or the quality of the farmland and wildlife habitats that were being destroyed.

In recent years government policies have swung away from support for private enterprise and Sitka spruce monoculture in favour of conservation and the removal of these same spruce plantations. Forestry Enterprise (as the agency is known these days) now has to fulfil its timber quotas, manage sustainable forests, encourage recreation and conserve and enhance wildlife habitats.

In the late 1960s, I was advised by a schools careers officer to apply for a job in the Forestry Commission, because it was an industry with a future and I had told him I wanted to work out of doors. He gave me a leaflet which said I needed a maths 'O' level for the FC, so there was never much chance of me becoming a forestry officer. However, I was impressed by books like the *The Living Forest* and *The Seasons and the Woodman*, in which foresters appeared straight and strong, wise and a little magical, just like trees. Why they needed a maths 'O' level I never discovered.

If you look in the backyards of antique shops you often see rusting farm implements and tools, among which may be double-handed cross-cut saws, once the stock-in-trade of real woodmen who were employed as contract workers by the FC or local estates. These forest workers were taken on for particular tasks like planting or felling and the rest of the time they had to find other employment, as rabbit-catchers, fencers and labourers. Their wisdom was of a very down-to-earth kind.

I walked up the Breamish Valley with Jim Givens recently, and he pointed to blocks of conifers planted with his father fifty years ago, then showed me the cross-cut saw they had used in their work; 7 feet of steel and a sculpted row of glittering fangs. Laying-in with an axe, then setting yourself with the saw, bending your back to the pull stroke, felling tree after tree, must have been a tough way to earn a living.

Harvesters and Horse Work

I know of no-one who fells trees with an axe or a hand-saw these days – it is a task consigned to history with no regrets. But with the advance of Sitka forests from Rothbury to Kielder, there is still a lot of work for contractors. They now drive 'harvesters' worth a quarter of a million pounds that can cut and process 15 tonnes of log poles per hour. The first time I saw one of these machines in action I was impressed by the combination of power and dexterity. The operator never had to leave his cab, get wet or scrape resin from his hands. Neither was he going to be crippled with lumbago or sciatica by the time he was fifty.

The Beniams boys, Paul and Jonathan, working in the woods near Sewingshields.

Modern harvesters and forwarders can only work effectively on level ground where the job on hand is to clear-fell extensive plantations. To thin existing woodland where there is an ecological or amenity interest, Forest Enterprise has copied the practice of conservation agencies, employing freelance woodmen using horses which can get in among standing trees on steep ground.

Far from being just a quaint or nostalgic way of getting the task done there is hard-nosed economy in horse work. Each contractor has to cut the timber by chain-saw or pay someone else to do so, then rope up his or her horse to haul each log out onto an access track, where it can be hitched onto a logging arch or loaded onto a pole wagon. Every log is measured to assess its metric weight. The contractor is paid according to the wood he can sell. Most of the equipment or machinery for this horse-work comes from Scandinavia, where they use both traditional and modern forestry methods and have some of the most beautiful managed woods in Europe.

The horses are home-grown and in Northumbria most of them seem to be Clydesdales from southern Scotland. As one of the Kielder woodmen told me: 'You can't talk to a machine, but you can always have a conversation with your horse.'

Although some of the big conifer forests are home to special birds and animals like goshawks and red squirrels, it is the mixed broadleaved woodland that contains the wealth of Britain's wildlife and was the traditional source of timber and underwood, used for everything from tool-handles to fences and hurdles.

In Northumbria many smaller woods were managed as coppice with standards and in some places, like the Allen Valley, this system is being reintroduced. At Chopwell Woods in Gateshead there is a woodland weekend each year when tradition crafts are demonstrated and you can see bodgers and charcoal burners at work. However, compared with Cumbria the woodland industries of Northumberland and Durham were never extensive and little has survived into contemporary culture. Yet people still like woods and take their children on nature walks.

When I was a student, woodland ecology was all about transects and chi squares. We did our fieldwork in a local wood where the Forestry Commission was clearing an area of birch. This meant we were able to indulge a healthy fascination with alcohol, tapping two sturdy birch trees and drawing off 5 gallons of sap to make some 'country wine'.

As we were carrying the demijohns out of the main ride we met a couple of foresters and for a few moments I thought we were in trouble – we had not seen the necessity of asking permission before vandalising the doomed trees. However, the only comment we got was a warning about the properties of birch sap wine: 'powerful openin' medicine,' they said, exchanging knowing glances. When in due course it had been boiled, racked and bottled, we left it for at least a week before trying it and coming to the conclusion that the foresters were right: it was dreadful. Four years later my wife Mary entered a bottle in the county WI competition and it won first prize – no mean accolade, but by then we only had a couple of bottles left.

A change of scale; Kielder Forest in Northumberland. The Locomo 990 Harvester will cut and trim up to 15 tonnes of wood an hour. This plantation, spruce with a little pine, is about fifty years old and it will be cleared and replanted in a year. Brashings will be gathered into a heap and young spruce trees planted between.

42

Peter Banks operating a harvester in Kielder Forest. The wood is sold either by direct contract or standing sales. Kielder District has 20 harvesters, costing £240,000 each, processing about 20,000 tonnes each. Most of the wood will go for pulp.

A big beast in Kielder Forest. A Hemek forwarder (made in Sweden, as is most forestry machinery) at work pulling out and stacking log poles.

Buster and Rosso pulling pole wagons in Kielder Forest. Not such big beasts but surprisingly efficient. Horses are used when the lie of the land is difficult or ecologically sensitive. Dave Campbell of Selkirk and Heinrick Jung of Moffat are freelance contractors, spending the summer at Kielder, paid for what they can process and sell. Every load is measured to calculate the metric weight and then led to an access point.

Heinrick Jung with Buster, his nine-year-old Clydesdale gelding, working in Kielder Forest.
A few months after the picture was taken I had a phone call from Heinrick's wife asking for
a special photograph of Buster, who had died quite suddenly. If Heinrick had driven a
forwarder would his wife have wanted to give him a picture of it for Christmas?

Dave Campbell and Rosso, taking a break in a sunny clearing, Kielder Forest in Northumberland. 'It looks a pretty life but in winter frosts with your finger frozen it's not so rosy.'

Dragging spruce poles out of the forest so they can be loaded onto a pole wagon. Dave Campbell and Rosso, Kielder Forest. There are trees for miles around in every direction. A few minutes after I took the photograph I was alone in the clearing when a roe buck ghosted out from the shadows less than 10 feet away.

FIVE

Traps and Tales

Knowing the secret lives of animals is essential if you are going to make a career out of killing them. Good keepers have to think like pheasants and foxes, which makes them interesting characters.

When I was writing a book called *The Cheviot Way of Life*, I talked to the mole-catcher Bill Grieve of Lilburn, who explained that in his work the secret was to smell like a mole. He meant that moles mistrusted unusual smells, so that to trap them in their tunnels you had to rub the aluminium traps with a dead mole to take the human smell away. However, at a publication launch at Ingram Village Hall the main press interest centred on Bill and what he smelled like. It made for an interesting day or two when the reviews came out but did little for my intention of trying to explain the subtleties of life on the land.

Years after the book came out I spent a couple of days with 'Bob the Mole' – Bob Sanderson of Chillingham – who always wore gloves to his work. When I asked him why he wore gloves he changed the subject and I realised he was reluctant, understandably, to say anything about smells. It was much later before a local estate worker told me that Bob was a smoker and moles did not like the smell of cigarettes. I have always had a great respect for moles: conservative and bad-tempered, but good at their job. By extension a successful mole-catcher has to be the same – but better.

A century ago, half of the Northumbrian fauna was considered vermin and churchwardens paid a set fee for the tails of badgers, otters, pole-cats and pine martens. At 4d. (2p) a time it is hardly surprising that some animals were driven to extinction. The puzzle is that so many were not. I can imagine the scene as unlikely bounty-hunters handed over their old tobacco tins full of stoat tails. A furtive business, but the idea of having to prove your skill or success at vermin control has continued into the twenty-first century in the way moles are sometimes still hung on wire fences and crows are strung up on gibbets. There are things about the countryside that have little to do with common sense and a lot to do with the way things have always been done.

Matt Avery, head gamekeeper of Shawdon, took me round his pheasant sheds one March afternoon and finished off by taking me down to the Shawdon Burn, a pretty tributary of the Aln. We walked along the banks of butterbur to see where his wild mallards were nesting. He had each nest marked and monitored but would not let us go too close. A female mallard is beautifully camou-flaged and will sit very tight. According to Matt, a fox could walk past her without seeing her, but if she was disturbed the fox would scent her straight away. This seemed to me to be knowledge borne of experience.

When we went down to the burn to check a mink trap, Matt said you had to keep trapping mink because they were taking over the river catchment and would kill everything. Mink are territorial, and I had heard that if you removed one there was a chance you would attract two or three to fill the gap. But I was not inclined to contradict Matt. It was his patch and his livelihood. Also, I had seen the devastation caused by mink to nesting common sandpipers and oystercatchers.

The Pheasant's Only Friend

The essential task of a keeper is to raise game birds. Shooting has become a lucrative business for landowners and is no longer a sport necessarily reserved for family and friends. An estate might have four or five shoots a month but all but one of these might be let to syndi-cates. If people pay large amounts of money to shoot pheasants then they expect there to be a lot more of them shoot, which means that there is more pressure on keepers to raise more and more chicks.

Twenty years ago I visited the Chipchase estate on the North Tyne, where Matthew Blair showed me his incubators and described the tricky business of hatching pheasants and transferring them to 'artificial hens'. Today, Matthew's way of doing things is considered 'traditional' or eccentric: most estates buy in chicks or poults and give them little time in the release pens before turning them out into the woods. Which is why there seem to be so many more pheasants loafing around road verges and why they have such little common sense. Getting eaten by foxes or run over on country roads is acceptable wastage: enough will survive for each syndicate day. Whether these dozy young pheasants offer much sport is another matter.

When you have spent your life learning how to be a good gamekeeper it must be disheartening to see the job done badly. When I asked Denis Smailes, head keeper of Harehope, what he thought of the way things were changing he was particularly dismissive of the trend towards big estates and let days. 'If you just release birds you don't need to control vermin. Keepers then are just poultrymen.'

Pheasants belong in Asia and the Far East and were not introduced into Britain until Saxon times. At first they were raised for food rather than sport and were a centrepiece of royal banquets, along with cranes and peacocks. When they became feral is a mystery, but one of the earliest literary references to wild pheasants comes from a version of the Northumbrian ballad about the Battle of Otterburn (i.e. Chevy Chase) in 1388. So there must have been keepers rearing pheasants around here over 600 years ago. When the handsome ring-necked variety was introduced into Britain in the eighteenth century, it was from the Duke of Northumberland's estate at Alnwick that they were first released. Pheasants go back a long way in this part of the world.

Recently I called in at Harehope to see Denis Smailes again: still head keeper and with just as much pride in his work. Although he takes his pheasants seriously he has a particular soft spot for partridges – the native greys rather than the red-legs. Grey partridges have become scarce at Harehope and no one is allowed to shoot them any more. When I first met Denis ten years ago he was rearing grey partridge chicks, keeping them in release pens for several weeks before letting them out to augment any wild ones around Old Bewick. The estate gave up doing this because the partridges proved far too clever. 'The little beggars wouldn't stay at home,' says Denis. 'After one or two shoots they got into one big pack and then... whoosh!'

Day-old grey partridges are a delight – highly-strung and always busy, 'like grey bumblebees.'

Rearing pheasants at Harehope in Northumberland. The 'electric hen' keeps the ten-day-old chicks safe and warm (they need to be 70–75° F) and the rounded piece of board in the background stop them getting lost in the corners.

Denis Smailes, head keeper at Harehope in Northumberland, holding pheasant chicks. This picture always makes me smile because of the sticking plasters: 'Chapped keens,' said Denis, ' – diesel's bad for them.'

Denis Smails with his poults in the release pens. He whistles to bring the seven-week-old poults in to feed. At this age they are given pellets rather than crumb, reducing the protein level all the time. Denis will visit them three times a day, starting at 5.30am.

Pheasant poult in the release pen at Harehope.

Beaters gathering for the shoot at Harehope. Most are regulars, like Bob Steward (third from right), coxswain of Amble lifeboat and a staunch 'countryman'.

Guns returning after a partridge shoot: the Long Strip on the Harehope estate.

After the shoot, the reckoning. Guests on a shoot get a brace to take away: the rest are sold. Anne Wrangham, wife of estate-owner Ted Wrangham, is talking to keeper Denis and his son Richard. The dog is Old Zena. Ten years ago pheasants were worth £3 a brace, which went a long way towards paying the beaters. There are so many pheasants shot now that the value has fallen to 25p.

The last of the grey partridges released into the stubble fields above the River Till: New Bewick Farm in the distance, near Edlingham in Northumberland.

Vermin control on the banks of the River Breamish in Northumberland. Richard Smailes is holding a trap containing a live mink, soon to be shot.

Outlaws on parade: a keeper's gibbet near Shawdon. The two animals on the left are mink (the usual form is chocolate-brown, but a few are silver, as in the one second left). Third on left is a female stoat, then a pair of weasels and on the right are two moles.

Bob Sanderson of Chillingham digging a square pit to set a mole trap in the lambing field at Harehope in Northumberland. It seemed when I took this photograph in April 1995 that aluminium traps would soon be a thing of the past: most mole-catchers had changed to strychnine-covered worms as an easier method of control. But strychnine is more difficult to obtain now, and in any case, mole-catchers like to see their efforts have been rewarded. It is only when you see a field covered with molehills that you appreciate why farmers are happy to pay to have the moles killed.

Setting a mole trap. Bob Sanderson ('Bob the Mole') wears gloves to lessen his scent. Traps are only ever cleaned by rubbing off the soil – they are never washed or oiled.

A mole trap, set and in place but not yet covered. A square of turf is cut using a small notched spade. The trap is bedded onto the mole run and firmed down, then loose soil is spread over the top. The turf square is left as a marker. The next day it will be obvious from the visible wire if a mole has been caught.

The main mole runs are usually around the edges of fields, leading to and from water. Moles are fierce and solitary creatures and each animal will have its own territory, but the main runs are shared. Bob Sanderson with his kit – a string of traps and spade, setting a trap in a main run of the lambing field, Harehope in Northumberland.

A 'two-dog trap' – i.e. two male moles caught in the same trap.

An old mole hanging on a roadside fence, like a crucifix.

Bob Sanderson, pleased with his morning's work, whistling on his way across the lambing field. 'That'll stop you coughing in church!', he said after finding two moles caught in the same trap.

A damp winter morning on the Lilburn estate. Bill Grieve bringing in his mole traps – the line of 20 traps has caught a dozen moles still held fast in the wires.

SIX

Lucky Heather

According to my copy of the *Observer's Book of Birds* (1952 edition), the red grouse is the only British bird found nowhere else in the world: our only indigenous species. Alas, by the time I bought the third volume of *The Birds of the Western Palaearctic* in 1980, the red grouse had been demoted to a subspecies of the Scandinavian hazel grouse and there was nothing unique about Britain at all.

This is hardly surprising as our island was only created a few thousand years ago – not enough time for new species to evolve. In fact, the red grouse had been ecologically-isolated from the rest of northern Europe long before the severing of the land bridge. The moorland of 'Atlantic' Britain must have been a world on its own, where the white-winged hazel grouse was not ideally suited and a dark-winged form appeared: not a new species but well on the way to being a little bit different. So there is something moderately special about our grouse after all, which makes it a very British bird.

When I first took an interest in wildlife and wild places, the Pennine moors were a big attraction. In late April I watched the territorial battles of green hairstreak butterflies and listened to curlews; in June I found grey chi and glaucous shears moths camouflaged on the drystone walls, and in late August I sat in the warm fug of heather scent and listened to bumblebees. I do not remember noticing grouse but they must have been there.

It was years later before I realised that the two were synonymous, that extensive heather moors could only exist if they had been managed for grouse and that grouse could only thrive if a contrived set of conditions was maintained. Over several centuries the indulgence of sporting landowners has created a glorious and unique habitat: conservation in order to kill things: a very British paradox. Edward Wilson of the Antarctic spent a decade studying grouse disease and turned down an invitation to go for the South Pole with Ernest Shackleton because his work was not finished. A few years later he went with Scott and died in the famous frozen tent, perhaps wishing he was back home with the grouse. In the 1910s Wilson was a celebrity, a gifted wildlife artist and a good shot. But although many of his friends were sportsmen and he loved the moors he did not feel comfortable in killing things for enjoyment. Neither pro or anti: another British paradox and one that reflects my own feelings.

Managing the Moors

Managing a viable heather moor is a full-time job for a team of keepers. The test of success is the number of grouse on the moor when shooting starts in August, but to achieve this there is a year of effort to create suitable feeding and breeding conditions. Vermin have to be controlled. In the past this meant pole-traps and poisoned bait to kill birds of prey but these are now illegal and most keepers know the law.

I have talked with a dozen keepers and they all have a different response to how they feel when a hen harrier appears on their moor. The comment that most impressed me came from a Teesdale keeper who said harriers were a threat to his livelihood, but he then spent five minutes giving me a detailed description of watching one hunt – 'bright as a button and like a petal on the breeze.'

However, lamping for foxes, shooting crows and trapping stoats are all part of the keeper's craft, carried out quietly and efficiently through the year. By the breeding season there are few natural enemies on a grouse moor. On the Pennines this benefits curlews and other wading birds as well as grouse: a managed moor is always bursting with life.

For suitable nest sites, and places to hide from predators, grouse like heather a foot or two in height, but for food they need new shoots, fresh and low. Thus one of the most important and visible tasks on a moor is to create a mosaic of different-aged heather. This is done by controlled burns, usually in March and early April when the ground is suitably dry. It may look a simple matter of setting a match to tinder but if you only want a 50-yard strip everything has to be carefully planned.

The first time I got close to a heather burn, at Midgy Ha' near Rothbury, I was astonished that it all started and stopped exactly where it was supposed to. The following year at Hagdon Moor, I took more notice of how much preparation was involved: first the head keeper Denis Smailes listened to the 5.30am shipping forecast for a guide to what the wind would do, then he phoned the police to tell them where he was likely to be working (this to avoid the embarrassment of a fire-brigade call-out). Once on the moor it was a question of seeing how the burn would stop once it had been started, then swiping a firebreak and backburning this before setting the main burn to work with the wind.

From close quarters, a moor fire is a frightening sight. All you have to control it is a beater or besom. The flames can be 8 feet high and swirling smoke always seems to be in your face. On the morning I was at Hagdon the wind started from the south-west but then veered through 90 degrees, steadying to create eddies and whirlwinds of flying soot. 'That's put a fair bit smoke down into Charlton,' said Denis. 'If Nancy Armstrong's got her washing out she'll no be best pleased.' In fact, I have been 2 miles from a burn and had my clothes ruined by a gentle black rain of heather ash.

Having spent so much time on the moors but at a spiritual distance from the guns, I decided I should see at least one grouse shoot at close quarters. It took some time to arrange but eventually I was invited to a shoot near Killhope in Weardale and spent two mornings there with the new keeper Nick Walmsley. My notes for the first morning were meant to remind me of what happened but they reflect a degree of confusion:

At lodge 8.30. Introduced to 'the Boss' and a few of his guests. Into vehicles with beaters and up to the moor. Three drives. Rain at start, gusting from north-west. Jess the springer intent and excited, as was flagman: very enthusiastic when one of the guns shot birds with left and right. Third drive, downwind back, by far the best. Sat a few feet from a butt and had a grouse tumble out of the sky in front of me. 58 brace by lunch.

Without the killing there would be no heather moors, but I still found it an unsettling experience.

It seemed in the 1960s and '70s that the purple moors I knew well were destined to go wild, to become rank and threadbare as landowners lost interest in shooting and sheep grazing became an easy and less costly alternative to grouse management. By the late 1990s everything had changed, agriculture was at a low ebb and shepherds were being laid off.

Ambitious estates realised that heather could be lucky: shooting was one of the few growth industries and if they took the sheep off the blacklands heather would regenerate and the uplands could be a goldmine. Many landowners now fit in their own shoots when let days allow: the new generation of field sports enthusiasts live in cities and fly in for a day's entertainment. Things come around and go around, but never quite the same.

Burning heather, Hagdon Moor in north Northumberland.

Above: *Smoke and fire across Hogdon Moor.*
Richard Smailes beating down the edge of the
heather-burn. Everything is under control...

Denis Smailes and Bob Kinghorn, through
the white smoke of a moor-burn.

Keeper Nick Walmsley of Killhope in Upper Weardale, County Durham, digging out a stone shooting butt. An old butt can resemble an army trench: cold, wet and uncomfortable.

Nick Walmsley and Robert Mitchell building the wooden frame of a shooting butt: Upper Weardale.

The wooden frame of a shooting butt taking shape ready for the grouse season. A two-man job: Nick Walmsley and Robert Mitchell.

Beaters on a wet morning in late September, Killhope in Upper Weardale.

A flagman's task is to be as energetic and visible as possible, to persuade the grouse to fly towards the guns. The springer spaniel lends moral support.

Flagman on the flank: frantic waving stops the grouse veering away to left or right as a line of beaters walks towards the guns.

Moment of truth on a grouse shoot. One of the birds in the picture has been hit. Each butt accommodates a 'gun' and a loader.

A line of beaters closing in on the shooting butts, where the guns have fallen silent. The grouse have flown: October in Upper Weardale.

Trevor Green picking up after a grouse shoot, Upper Weardale, County Durham.

After the shoot, the keepers can smile – Nick Walmsley with Harry Beadle, head keeper of Eggleston.

SEVEN

Catchy Weather

Spring creeps slowly onto the high hills, inch by inch up burns and becks, along valley-shanks and over the black-lands. Flowering sallow and hazel yields to gorse and rowan. Emperor moths fly helter-skelter over the heather.

In the Cheviots it is late March before anyone thinks about lambing, and on the furthest farms, in the snow-shadow of the Border Ridge, it is the end of April before the first Blackface or Swaledale lamb is dropped. To be on the spot to the see the annual life-and-death struggle takes resolution, particularly if the weather is bad and you have other things you could be doing.

Low Bleakhope Farm is tucked out of the way in a twist of the Breamish, only accessible along a narrow private track from Hartside, which is itself a long way from the foot of the valley. I had to leave home at 5am to be at the farm in time to check the Cushat Law heft with Stuart Nelson, and because of the unpredictable light and the 'catchy' weather I had to repeat the process three times before I had any worthwhile photographs. I was never in time for a cup of tea, always a step behind Stuart and his collie (called Bill, and various other names), and always out of breath.

The slopes of Cushat Law and Shill Moor are so steep that a quad bike would be in constant danger of capsizing, so Stuart walks. From the farm-house a path leads past a barn and a bush, in which a ring ouzel always nests, through a gate and then straight up onto a shoulder of Cushat Law.

On a good day, the one I remember, we started in deep shade but soon climbed into diamond-bright sunshine. It was still cold and there was a dusting of frost in all the shadows, turning them blue against the bleached tussocks of mat-grass. 'When the moss rises the sheep can feed,' said Stuart, meaning that the fresh stems of the mat-grass were turning creamy at the base and the sheep could graze through the tough outer sheaths to find some food value. It was a late season and the green flush was only just under way.

We contoured around Cushat and onto Shill Moor; it took about four hours and most of the time we were walking through tussocks of mat-and moor-grass. Now and then Stuart would stop and shade his eyes to look across to the far sweep of hillside where strings of sheep were on the move. The collie worked the flocks so that they would graze back through the day. If any sheep was on its own, it probably meant it was lambing and we checked several to make sure they were all right. They usually were. Those with twins we pushed downhill ahead of us, to a stell or fold where they could be taken back to the inbye fields for better grazing. One forlorn ewe was having some difficulties with her second lamb and the first one did not look very lively, so Stuart scooped it up and put it in his bag to take it back to the farm to be 'set on'.

By the time we had finished back in the pens it was early afternoon and Stuart had half an hour's break before he had to repeat the whole process. I drove back down the valley, where swallows and sand martins were hawking for gnats over the river. I could hear the song of a willow warbler at Peggy Bell's Bridge and there were still some fieldfares in the paddock by Ingram Farm. Things were changing by the hour; the world's axis had tilted from winter into spring.

Willie Taylor and the Skunk House

A few miles south of Wooler, where the Harthope Burn escapes from the Cheviot's eastern foothills, is the hamlet of North Middleton. I sometimes called there to see Willie Taylor the fiddler.

Willie was always interested in where I had been and who I had been talking to among the local farm workers and shepherds. He had a fund of stories culled from his own long career as a shepherd in the College and Harthope valleys. These stories often included something scurrilous and I took them with a pinch of salt. I tried to steer the subject round to music, because I was trying to record some tunes with him for a National Park video.

Willie had lived at Low Bleakhope in the 1930s and his neighbour at High Bleakhope had been another respected fiddler called George Armstrong; the two played at local dances (payment was usually a bottle of whisky) and spent winter evenings together practising, sharing tunes and playing nap and dominoes.

Fame came late to Willie Taylor and too little of his music has made it onto CD. When I was trying to record some of his beautiful slow airs he admitted he had not played very much over the winter because of a bad back and a bad elbow, but he also had trouble remembering the starts to tunes ('There's plenty polkas,' he said, 'it's just minding 'em'). If he got the start right then the whole thing flowed beautifully. Otherwise he tut-tutted and got cross. At eighty, Willie could play like an angel, but he could be an old devil too.

One of Willie Taylor's tall stories involved what he called the Skunk House in the College Valley. According to Willie, two Germans had settled in a tiny cottage on the steep east slope of the valley and had built a set of cages for skunks. This had happened a few years before the Great War. Nobody knew where the Germans came from or where they eventually disappeared to, but the local word was that on dark nights they climbed the slopes of Newton Tors to flash signals to low-flying Zeppelins.

It sounded strange enough to be true and a few weeks later, I took Willie and Nancy up to the College Valley so we could walk up through the primroses to see if there was anything left of the Skunk House. According to my notebook the path led us:

…to Harra (or Hare?) Bog: into gnarled alder/hazel wood. Very open and grass growing rank now sheep are excluded. Found patch of narcissi which were in the garden of the Germans' hut. Foundations of hut covered in moss. Stone shelter or outhouse further north. No obvious sign of skunk house itself. Willie expecting to find the rabbit wire, and the rusty bed and armchair in the hut. Some very good hazel coppice which Willie had once cropped for walking stick shanks. He got very excited when we found some good straight poles: 'I'll come back in a year or two and that'll be a good 'un.' Then down the track looking for old plum trees, now gone. This the first time Willie or Nancy had been in the College Valley since they'd left Southern Knowe in '58. Willie says they should never have left. 'It was a good berth. But the slopes were steep.'

Willie described himself as a player of dance music rather than a traditional folk musician, and he had no time for the 'folk revival', or most current fiddlers whose bowing techniques were not up to his standard. When he died, in November 2000, the Guardian ran a six-column obituary (written by Alistair Anderson) and it still makes me smile to think of Willie's life story given top billing ahead of politicians and industrialists.

Setting out on the second lap of Cushat Law in the High Hills of the Cheviot. Hill lambing in early May: Stuart Nelson of Low Bleakhope with his collie Bill.

Any ewe with twins has a tough time in the High Hills. One of this Swaledale's lambs is sickly so Stuart Nelson decides to take it down to the farm where it can be 'set on' with another ewe. After catching it he puts it in his bag. A shepherd always carries a bag slung over his shoulder – it contains useful items like twine, disinfectant and a marking stick.

Stuart Nelson takes a mid-morning break after four hours of 'looking' the Cushat Law heft.
The lamb seems happy enough in the bag and Bill the collie enjoys some attention.

A sheep stell (a stone-walled circular fold) in the Upper Breamish Valley near Bleakhope.
Stuart Nelson loads a ewe and lamb into the trailer of his quad bike to take them back to
the farm.

Stuart Nelson skinning a dead lamb. If a lamb dies it means there is a ewe with milk to spare: she might make a foster-parent for a sickly lamb brought down from the hill. However, she will reject the lamb if it smells unusual, so the dead lamb's skin is drawn over the lamb to be adopted. Setting on a lamb, as this is called, does not always work; the ewe sometimes refuses to take the substitute.

Michael Jameson of West Hotbank Farm near Haltwhistle, with a lamb ready to set on.
The dead lamb's skin (which will soon attract flies) will be removed when the ewe accepts
the replacement.

Lambing a Cheviot ewe at Sillywrea Farm. Sheep usually manage perfectly well on their own, but sometimes they need help. John Dodd holds the ewe while his daughter Frances pulls the lamb clear and checks it can breathe properly.

Frances and Richard Wise of Sillywrea Farm carrying lambs out of the yard to lead a Suffolk ewe to a nearby paddock. In the background is Monty the Clydesdale.

Cheviot lambs head-banging while their mother gets on with the serious business of transforming grass into milk to feed them.

Willie Taylor, retired Cheviot shepherd and one of the finest fiddlers in Britain. His left index finger was lost to a turnip-chopper when he was a boy.

Maurice Toward with shovel and divining rods for replacement of a field drain, Herdship Farm in Upper Teesdale.

EIGHT

Ditches and Dykes

I reap and I mow and I harrow and sow,
Sometimes a hedging and ditching I go;
No work comes amiss, for I thresh and I plough,
Thus my bread I do earn by the sweat of my brow

The Nobleman and the Thresher

Early June and the first sunny morning of the year. Teesdale was alive with sound and colour and Maurice Toward was relaying a field drain in the saddle of meadows beside Herdship Farm. 'See l'al tewits standin'?' said Maurice, pointing out a clutch of downy lapwings, stock-still like lichen-covered stones in the grass. Redshanks were calling from fence-posts, skylarks were singing from somewhere overhead. It really was a glorious day.

Upper Teesdale is famous for its flowers and birds: farming created the habitats but modern methods have proved too efficient, too destructive of the environment. English Nature is trying to get the balance right but many of the local farmers resent the interference. Maurice was pragmatic, proud of his lapwings but also determined to manage an effective farm to the benefit of all, which seems to me to be the right way to farm. When the 'maister-drain' stopped working, waterlogging the field, he made plans to dig it out.

Banks of bird's-eye primrose and globeflower flanked a marshy basin of cuckoo-flower and meadow saxifrage. When we reached the green hollow of the meadow we found David Bainbridge already pacing out the slope, to get the fall of level right. David is a farm contractor, profoundly deaf but greatly respected by local farmers for his skill in ditching work. 'He'll always do a hundred-per-cent job,' said Maurice. 'He'll set to and eye the field and can tell straight off the lie of the drains and how old each pipe is. When you work with him you soon understand him.'

The only tricky part of the day's work was to find the exact line of the master drain – the underground channel all the side-drains fed into.

Two hundred years ago most of the land in any northern parish was waterlogged and waste. It was only by hand-digging drains in efficient herringbone patterns that rainwater could be carried off quickly enough to make the land sweet. It took generations to dry out the marshes and bogs destined to be our countryside. Farmers and ditching boys maintained the system; the old tile drains often needed repair.

Maurice had taken on Herdship from his uncle and knew the ground well, but it was still difficult for him to visualise the hidden pattern beneath our feet. To find the master drain, Maurice produced a pair of divining rods – two bent lengths of galvanised wire. I was sceptical but impressed by his confidence. He had learned divining from 'the Old People', and within a few minutes, by walking to and fro at different angles, he had pinpointed where the water lay – the spot to dig.

I tried the rods myself, letting the wires lie loose but firm, the short lengths vertical and the long lengths swinging horizontally between thumbs and forefingers. At first nothing happened, but then quite suddenly the rods were working, crossing as I paced over a tussock of round-rush, and crossing in the same place when I set off from a different angle. I still have no idea how divining works, but I know that it does.

When David had finished digging the narrow trench – using a shovel and his back-actor digger on a Massey-Ferguson tractor – the two of them shovelled gravel around the new drainage pipe. The job was soon done. Within a few weeks it would be hard to see where they had been, but the ground would dry out better, yield fewer rushes and more fescue, and be a little less attractive to marsh flowers and waders.

Stone on Stone

Most tasks around a farm, like reaping and sowing, threshing and ploughing, are now the business of the tractorman. A very few jobs take just as long to do today as they did a century ago. Drystone walling is one of them. Like ditching it was hard work, and it still is. In hill-farming areas walls or dykes have made as big a visual contribution to the uplands as hedges have to the lowlands. People like to see drystone walls making order out of chaos; stone on stone.

Last summer I climbed the path from Bellingham to Shitlington and noticed a wall I had seen built ten years ago had been badly dented by a tractor. Among the teetering facing-stones were clumps of thyme and rock-rose, and in the hollow core was what looked like shredded cardboard but turned out to be a wasp nest. A closer look revealed it had been raided by a badger – one of the few creatures with a thick enough skin to ignore wasp stings. Drystone walls have a story to tell beyond their working life. Under normal circumstances they last for centuries and become a home to a lot of wildlife.

The function of walls, to separate stock from crops and mark out owner-ship, has changed over the years and there is no practical need for many of the old boundaries, certainly on the high hills of Durham and Northumberland. Like hedges they are surplus to requirement, but rather remove them they are left to crumble in their own time, in the place they

belong. After all, the stones may have already been reused several times over, from Bronze Age cairns to sheilings and hogg-houses; they are a resource available when necessary. For the moment, derelict walls are a feature of the countryside: a generation of walkers has learned to accept them as part of the scene. But on any working farm a number of walls still do an essential job and have to be maintained.

Small gaps in a wall are easily mended by a farmer, but the days of having seasonal Irish labour on hand to rebuild a mile-long dyke are long gone. This means there is a role for a modern sort of itinerant labourer, or for gangs of skilled workmen. Recently, the support of conservation agencies and European funding has meant there has been enough contract work to keep experienced teams together for months at a time, with only seasonal breaks for other farm work.

Dismantling an old wall is like taking apart a three-dimensional jigsaw – it is essential to place the components to hand so they can be put back in the right order. On the occasions I have watched a walling gang I have been struck by the organisation involved.

Tom Arres of Kelso, who had been a waller in the Cheviots for thirty years, held a conversation with me one morning without taking his eyes off his half-built dyke. As he talked he tested and measured – by eye and touch – the shape and weight of every stone laid out on the ground parallel with the footings. He ran his hands under and around each piece in turn, rearranging the order, working out how they would fit together so they would only need to be handled once. While his son and the rest of the team were busy placing stone on stone, Tom was thinking several moves ahead.

I met a waller in the vastness of Moor House one day who had cleared a 10-yard stretch out of a long run of dyke, taking it down to the broad footings and rebuilding it to about waist height. He was working alone – he had been the only living soul I had met all day – and the only equipment he had with him was a broom. I never thought at the time to ask him why he needed a broom and our conversation was brief. It was a wet day – both of us were soaked – and it was late. What I remember most clearly was his hands. Like Tom Arres he was feeling the stones as he worked, and his hands were leathery and padded, like wicket-keeper's gloves.

In the Pennines and south Northumberland all walls are built of sandstone. When the Romans built their most famous of walls they used local sandstone even though the rock at their feet along the Whin Sill was dolerite, which could not be worked and was only any use as infill or rubble between the facings.

Sandstone has cleavage planes; it can be shaped into squared slabs and there are longer pieces that can be used as 'through-stones' to keep the structure stable. In the Cheviots there is no sandstone – all the available rock, whether river-washed boulders or from weathered outcrops, is volcanic. This calls for a different approach to wall build-ing. As George Hall of Rothbury told me: 'you can't argue with whin boulders.' Round boulders do not lend themselves to arranging in tiers or layers and it is a case of letting the two faces lean in on each other, allowing their weight to lock the whole thing together. A wall can be a yard thick at the base and a yard and a half high, so each yard in length weighs about a ton.

A man builds 4 yards of wall in a day, so a lifetime can be measured in a landscape.

David Bainbridge digging a trench for a field drain on Herdship Farm. Machinery can only get you so far – for the delicate or marshy bits you have to resort to a shovel.

Maurice Toward and David Bainbridge laying a drain: Herdship Farm in Upper Teesdale, County Durham. The plastic pipe has holes in it to let water seep into it from the surrounding ground. As the pipe is set in place it is bedded into gravel to help the water-flow.

The Arres walling team at Middleton Old Town near Wooler: Tom and Mark Arres, Jim Young and Grant Morrison. In the North Pennines many of the walling contractors work on their own, but in Northumberland most of the work is done by small teams.

Drystone walling in the Cheviot Hills. A wooden frame with a plumb-line is used as a template at the wall-end. Strings then mark the correct width for any given height. All the stone from the old wall is set out on the ground so Tom Arres can judge how it should go together: a three-dimensional jigsaw of unyielding andesite boulders. Middleton Old Town, Wooler in Northumberland.

Tom Arres of Kelso at work on a drystone wall at Middleton Old Town.

Thomas, George and Tom Hall walling at Park Hall Farm near Harbottle in Northumberland. Mid-May and perfect weather for outdoor work: dry with a cool north-easterly breeze.

Thomas Hall caressing facing-stones into place. In fact, these big sandstone blocks are brutally heavy and it often takes two people to set them into position.

In the Cheviots the available stone is andesite or granite, almost impossible to work and without any obvious facing or through-stones. Robin Cowans at Middle Dean in the Breamish Valley, Cheviot Hills.

Richie Jameson bringing in sheep to West Hotbank Farm, north of Hadrian's Wall in Northumberland: late afternoon, the sun low and the air damp.

NINE

Summer Gather

From lambing time to high summer, hill sheep are left to their own devices. They are 'looked' twice a day, but as long as there is enough bite in grass and heather the ewes will raise their lambs without much need of help. Then comes clipping and cowing, dipping and dosing, 'spaining' and sorting; for two or three months sheep are being shifted to and from the pens, making it a busy time for shepherds and dogs.

This is when good working dogs earn their keep. Some farmers and shepherds breed their own dogs and sell them part-trained to their neighbours, but it takes a lot of patience and dedication to be midwife and nursemaid to a collie. Ounce for ounce collies are the most temperamental, highly-strung and wilful of dogs. I have learned not to turn my back on one. A collie's natural instinct is to herd anything that moves, including you when you are walking through a farmyard; a nipped ankle is meant to guide you on your way.

Gathering sheep is usually done in the cool of the morning. A heft of sheep may be spread far and wide and be some distance from the farm, so a gathering day means an early start. Quad bikes are now universal and they can be great fun to ride, but they are probably the reason why several shepherds I know have put on a stone in weight over the past few years. Until the 1960s many Cheviot shepherds did their rounds on horseback, often from a pensioned-off hunter or fell pony. Gwen Wallace of Fulhope in Coquetdale is one of the few shepherds still using a horse instead of a quad bike. She breeds collies too and clearly has a knack with animals. But at the end of a gather most shepherds would rather have breakfast than brush down a horse.

Watching a gather is best done from a far hillside. Whenever I have kept pace with a shepherd it has been a confusing affair of whistles and shouts as the dog (or dogs) have been sent off to push the flock one way or another. '"Come by" means go left, "away" means go right and "that'll do" means "that'll DO!"' said Stuart Nelson when I asked what the standard dog instructions were. This was on a sultry July morning on Cushat Law when one of Stuart's dogs, Bill, was being troublesome. A few months later Bill was exiled to Lincolnshire: a working dog is only as good as its last gather.

Sheep rarely go the way you expect, which is why it is better to get a general view of the whole rake of a hill. What at first seems like twos and threes of sheep stop-starting and cutting back on the blind side resolves itself into a trickle and then a stream of ewes and half-grown lambs following each other along sinuous tracks. These tracks braid and converge until suddenly a whole cut of 200 sheep is behaving as a unit, with the dogs trailing the flanks and the shepherd at the back. At least, that is what ought to happen: the dogs get the blame if anything goes wrong.

Sheep pens always look complicated but they are simply a set of holding compartments linked by gates with a shedder. Sheep are channelled into a 'race' about 2 feet wide which leads them to a gate; this is then swung one way or the other by the shepherd to divert them left or right into different paddocks. Once separated they can be dealt with as necessary. On many farms the shedder was housed in its own low building, open at the far side so that the sheep were attracted forward. Sometimes, the whole set of pens is now under cover so the sheep can be kept dry.

The main reason for bringing sheep to the pens in the middle of summer is to shear or 'clip' them. These days this is often done by contract labour, sometimes local lads but possibly from as far afield as New Zealand. Teams start in June and work their way from farm to farm up the valleys. Each shearer can deal with about 200 sheep in a day – hard physical work. Sometimes, as at Bowlees in Teesdale where the Pike Law stints are some distance from the farm, a generator has to be taken out to the moor where temporary folds are set up and the whole shearing process takes place in the open air. That is if the weather is kind.

Clipping and Dipping

My only experience of clipping a sheep was on Hotbank Farm, where I had been photographing Michael Jameson as he rounded up a few strays at the end of a shearing day. All the electrical clippers had been cleared away so he dealt with the strays by hand, using dagging

Strings of sheep heading south from East Hotbank across the rolling 'cuesta' land-scape north of Hadrian's Wall. One of the dots in the far distance is Michael Jameson on his quad bike.

shears. This made a good picture but at the end of it he insisted we swap jobs.

There was only one ewe left and it was scruffy before I started. Fortunately, I already knew that the trick with sheep is to treat them like small children and be masterful. It sat still, in a heap, forlorn and sheepish, while I hacked at its greasy fleece and left it with several nasty cuts and grazes. Michael enjoyed the entertainment, but I persevered. My own satisfaction – at seeing the results of his photography – came later.

A sheep's fleece is a cosy habitat for all sorts of creatures apart from the sheep. Sheep are martyrs to ticks, flukes, headflies, scab and a thousand other pests and diseases, and for centuries people have tried their best to find effective remedies for their ailments. In the 1800s the five-star treatment was to force sheep through a river crossing and then massage their fleeces with butter and tar or molasses. Forty years ago things had progressed to a dip in organochlorine pesticides, which were then emptied into watercourses, with disastrous consequences for otters and everything else in the food chain. At present, most sheep are still dipped once or twice in the late summer, with organophosphorus pesticides which are not so harmful to wildlife, and farmers are not allowed to dump the waste in the nearest river. Even so, dipping seems a primitive ritual.

Sheep may not be very bright but you can see them pursing their lips and holding their noses as they are prodded into a Diazinon dip. I am sure they would support a more widespread use of pour-ons and sprays. Getting close enough for a good picture of the dipping pit at Brieredge Farm I had to squat low among the dripping ewes, which gave me a taste, literally, of what they had to endure in the name of personal hygiene. On the credit side, after a shower of pesticide I never suffered from ticks or scab for the rest of the summer.

While sheep are being sorted in the pens, a farmer will usually take the opportunity to dose them, using a worm and fluke drench, with a mineral supplement like cobalt to counterbalance the deficiencies of a wet-pasture diet. Again, the sheep show every sign of not liking it – they clamp up their jaws and turn their heads away at the last moment. It can only be because they remember the taste from last time. When they are eventually driven back up to the hill it must be a relief all round, but the shepherd then has the job of gathering another cut and going through it all again.

Driving sheep up the nick to Queen's Crags, north of the Wall. Michael Jameson of West Hotbank Farm checks to see if there are any stragglers as they head west for the farm.

Dick, Greg and Darren Dalton in the sheep pens at Wellhope Farm in mid-June. The rowan bush is only just into leaf; this is the highest farm in Weardale and summer is short. The small walled area contains a sheep dip and a shedder as well as open working pens.

The June gather is to dose the sheep against fluke and worm, vaccinate them, make sure they carry a keel mark, put castrating rings on male (wether) lambs and ear marks on female (gimmer) lambs. The wether lambs are fattened to be sold but many of the gimmer lambs will be replacements for the farm's flock. A gimmer lamb becomes a gimmer hogg when it is a year old. When it is clipped for the first time it becomes a shearling. Dick, Greg and Darren Dalton of Wellhope Farm in Upper Weardale, County Durham.

Dick Dalton hand-clipping an 'unkert' or stray Swaledale ewe in the yard of Wellhope Farm, Upper Weardale. All Dick's sheep are Swaledales and he is proud of them. When I asked him what he thought of Scotch Blackface he was scathing: 'Imagine waking up in the morning, going to the window and seeing all those daft faces staring back at you…'

Stuart Nelson of Low Bleakhope in the Cheviot Hills, driving in a cut of Swaledales along the ancient Salters Road.

Gwen Wallace, shepherd at Fulhope in Upper Coquetdale, with Molly and Meg.

Gwen Wallace bringing in sheep to the pens at Fulhope in Upper Coquetdale. This was one of Molly the old cob's last gathers – she was twenty-three and soon to be retired. The collie is Misty – Meg had pups and was not yet allowed back to work.

Steely light, hazy sunshine and a good morning for Malcolm Walton of Bowlees Farm to clip the 100 Swaledales on his stint at Pike Law Common in Upper Teesdale. The sheep are run on this wide exposed plateau to improve the heather for grouse management; this land is owned by the Raby estate. The climate is usually inhospitable: 'We leave a good tail on the sheep,' said Malcolm, 'so you don't leave the back door open when they're arse t't' wind…' Clyde's dog was playing games, letting the clipped sheep wander away before bringing them back to the area behind the fold.

Clipping in the pen on Pike Law Common: Clyde Barker and Malcolm Walton of Bowlees in Teesdale.

Malcolm Walton of Bowlees Farm in Teesdale, cleaning the shears in the clipping pen on Pike Law Common. He has taken off his boots to work on a rolled-out piece of carpet.

Dipping Blackface sheep at Brieredge Farm near Bellingham in Northumberland.

Birkdale Farm, Upper Teesdale, 1995.

TEN

Birkdale Clipping Day

On the footpath from Cauldron Snout to High Cup Nick, one of the most beautiful and remote landscapes in England, you pass a little stone farmhouse called Birkdale. Out of sight and sound of public roads, Birkdale is as close to the middle of nowhere as you can get. I must have walked past it once or twice in the 1980s without noticing it.

However, in 1992 when I was trying to take some pictures for an AA book I found myself waiting in the rain while the farmer and his wife worked a bunch of Swaledales into one of the pens beside the track. I was in no hurry – the bad weather was in for the day – and Mary and Brian Bainbridge invited me in for a cup of tea.

I have always been shy of imposing myself on people. At times this may have been a disadvantage in photography, but over the years it has also worked in my favour. It is better to be invisible when you are pointing a camera at people; farmers in particular do not respond well to being told what to do.

At Birkdale that wet afternoon the television was on and I remember having a conversation with Mary Bainbridge ranging from Brian Clough to Margaret Thatcher. We shared a fond regard for one (I grew up in Derby) and a strong dislike for the other. I think from then on Mary took me under her wing. If I wanted pictures of their farm, she said, I would have to come back another day and get in the way more. This suited me perfectly. The photographs I later got at Birkdale were the result of everyone knowing that Mary approved of my being there.

Most farming activities involve one person and a tractor. What once took gangs of labourers weeks of work – flailing corn, cutting hay, trimming hedges, hoeing turnips – now takes a specialist item of machinery a few hours. There are very few occasions when a farm can call its family and friends together to a seasonal task and a social gathering. I was particularly keen at Birkdale to be there on a clipping day. As far as I knew there were few Teesdale farms where the tradition was followed, where neighbours gave a day to each other to get a job done.

Brian was born and raised in Teesdale; Mary was from Dunston in Gateshead, but had lived in rural Durham since being evacuated there when she was nine. She had been a Land Girl at High Force, which may be how she met Brian. They had farmed at Birkdale ('Bir'dle') for many years, building up the flock to 900 (it was 'stinted' at 1200). Bad winters had taken their toll on the sheep, but they had never thought of giving up or moving.

I went to Birkdale's clipping day twice, in 1994 and 1995. The first time was so wet and dismal that I doubted any of the pictures would be much use, but in fact they told a compelling story. You could almost smell the damp wool and feel the water dripping down your neck. There were no sheltered pens at Birkdale, which meant the sheep got wet and clipping was difficult. My notebook reads:

Gang started after long wait with wet sheep. Shifted them from fold into hogg-house, then out again to get wind, then back in when it rained again. Clipped 420 in the byre by mid pm. Stopped for dinner 12.30. Sandwiches, pies, sausage rolls, trifle and a big mug of tea. Windows steamed over. Dogs, children everywhere. Watched TV for forecast. In and out again, but in the end they clipped the last 80 even though a bit wet: fleeces left out to dry rather than going into sacks. Children soaked catching little trout in the pool behind the farm.

For most of the day Brian had been absent, walking the 16 miles over High Cup to drive a heft and collect his strays: neighbouring farms exchange each other's lost sheep after the main gather:

Brian out about 04.30, walking over fell to Dufton. Drove 300 sheep back. Said they'd be tired at the end of it, so dogs having to work hard to keep them going. Rain at his back all day –

started as drizzle but turned to horizontal squalls. He looked half drowned when he got in. Round his neck a pair of shears tied by baling twine, in his pocket a bottle of whisky (from a neighbour across the fell, for his help there yesterday).

I should have taken a photograph of Brian when he got back from that long sheep drive, but he looked so weary that I left the image in my head and helped get him a cup of tea. After half an hour he was out into the rain again.

The following July could not have been a greater contrast. It was a wonderful sunny day and the clipping was all done outside. The two years demonstrated the highs and lows of hill farming, how it could crush your spirits or make them sing.

When I finally printed up the Birkdale pictures I sent a batch to the Bainbridges, and a few months later I got a note from Mary Bainbridge to say they had retired to Langdon Beck. The farm had been taken on by one of their daughters and the house was now the home of one of their grandsons, a gamekeeper. ' If you are ever over here just pop in to see us. Langdon Beck will tell you where we are. We still spend a lot of time at Birkdale. I have never really left.'

I kept the note intending to reply or visit, but I never did until a few months ago. Then, as instructed but seven years late, I called at the Langdon Beck Hotel and was directed to the Bainbridge's cottage in a field on the side of the fell. Mary was feeding the hens but Brian was out helping at the farm. We sat and shared stories for a few minutes and I heard all about the family and the farm. Out of the window I could see a blackcock sitting on the garden wall, and across the fell was the beckside where gentians would soon be in flower. A perfect Teesdale scene – but it was already spitting with rain.

Brian Bainbridge bringing in the High Cup gather along the route of the Pennine Way. Birkdale Farm, Upper Teesdale.

A sunny afternoon back at Birkdale after a long sheep-drive. The grass-covered trenches in the distance are 'hushes', created centuries ago by lead miners who dammed becks and then allowed the water to scour the fellside, exposing the lead veins.

Clipping outside in the sunshine, Birkdale 1995. Alison Mitchell (Brian and Mary Bainbridge's daughter) is putting the flock mark on a sheared Swaledale ewe.

Wet wool, sheep dung and cobwebs: Raymond Hutchinson clipping inside the old byre, Birkdale 1994.

Heather Kindleyside leading a clipped Swaledale ewe from the byre, Birkdale 1994.

Above: *The clipping team, Birkdale Farm, 1994: Susan Mitchell, Martin Mitchell, Lesley Mitchell, Martin Loxborough, Jacky Meeson, Susan Wilkinson, Mary Bainbridge, Andrew Bousfield, Ben Toward, Andrew Toward, Heather Kindleyside, Kevin Patterson, Dennis Rowland, Barry Meeson, Raymond Hutchinson, Paul Hutchinson, Tommy Bainbridge, Lee Stevenson, Becky Stevenson, Paul Rowland, Sandra Stevenson, Ryan Meeson.*

The clipping team 1995: this time with all the Bainbridge family in the picture, and the sun shining.

Jacky Meeson, eldest daughter of the Bainbridges, stitching up wool-sacks in Birkdale farmyard, 1995.

Stitching wool-sacks, in a horsebox to try to keep them dry, Birkdale 1994.

Relaxing after the clipping: Paul Rowland and Susan Wilkinson, Birkdale Farm, Upper Teesdale.

Bird nests in the open fields: oystercatcher, skylark and snipe.

A big bale in the corner of a June hayfield: a rare sight in Lower Weardale.

ELEVEN

Haying

Grass is taken for granted in temperate parts of the world – it just grows. But it only grows in the summer, which means that to keep livestock through the winter the grass has to be gathered and stored, either dry or 'pickled.'

I have seen old photographs of Cowshill in Weardale and Barrowburn in Coquetdale with lines of haystacks behind the stock sheds. Nobody today would dream of trying to grow a hay crop in the High Pennine or Cheviot valleys – hay is only as reliable as the weather.

In the Outer Hebrides, driving through Benbecula in the August of 1993, I noticed all the roadside fences had been draped with grass in a forlorn attempt to get it dry. At Loch na Faoilinn I stopped to talk to a crofter, Donald Ewan Macdonald, who was out with his wife stacking hay. The stacks were about 8 feet high, on wooden frames or trestles so the air could get through them, and roped or netted over so they did not blow away. Donald was proud of his stacks. They would stay out until September, then he would gather them together into a big thatched rick by the house. I marvelled at his patience, but in the Hebrides I doubt if he had much choice with stock to feed. It would have been the same in the Northumbrian hills until the 1950s.

The old way with hay was to graze the fields until late winter to let the manure fertilise the crop, then take the stock off and let nature take its course until June or July when the cut was taken. Wild flowers flourished under this system, because they could set seed before the harvest. The advent of artificial fertilisers changed things because the grass grew more aggressively and the flowers could not compete. So in a generation we have lost most of our pretty hay meadows in the interests of bigger grass yields.

In the Cheviots there are no 'traditional' meadows left, and in the North Tyne Valley there are probably only a dozen, despite attempts by the National Park Authority to encourage their conservation. In the North Pennines the East Allen is a beautiful valley but its fields are mostly 'improved.' It is only in Teesdale, through ESA designation and the efforts by English Nature, that flower-rich meadows have survived in sufficient numbers to make an impact on the landscape. A visit to Cronkley Farm or Widdybank in late June is one of the special pleasures of the Northumbrian summer – the fields are full of wood cranesbill, meadow saxifrage, march orchid, pignut, clover, eyebright and yellow rattle.

Every hill farm needs winter feed and every farmer tries to produce as much as possible without buying in more. Even heavily fertilised and productive hay crops can be lost in a wet summer, which is why silage is now so popular in the Upper Pennine valleys. When I asked Dick Dalton of Wellhope – the highest farm in Weardale – what the weather had been like in May he just sighed and said: 'It's like living in a piss-pot.' It had rained every day for three weeks. His chances of getting a hay harvest would have been negligible. Even his silage only yields a ton an acre, compared with 5 or 6 tons a few miles down the valley at Ireshopeburn.

Silage is cut earlier than hay, and after being left for a day to wilt it is simply rolled into big bales and wrapped in black plastic. The days of silage clamps and pits have given way to monumental rows of black bags. In country postcards they have taken the place of haystacks, and they will probably date the images in the same way.

Two Rows Up

To be involved in a 'proper' haying, I visited several Weardale and Teesdale farms, but it was at Sillywrea in Allendale, with John Dodd and his horses, that I came closest to pushing back the years and feeling the excitement and unpredictability of haymaking.

The weather forecast in the *Hexham Courant* had talked of a settled spell, and local farmers had taken a chance and cut early. So had John, who knew the risks of waiting. The hay needed two or three weeks from start to finish. 'Bad hay is made dearly,' said John; in a wet summer it might need to be turned three or four times and not be in until August, by which time there would be little food value in it.

This year was different. June came in dry, the swallows nested early and the hay-turners were busy only two or three days after the cut. The swaths were turned when the grass was more than half done, then turned again after a day to finish off.

When labour was easy, before the war, John remembers the haying as a time of endless effort. The swaths were gathered in by a horse-drawn paddy-sweep, then heaped into small 'kyles' which were considered safe to leave out in rain. After any rain, the kyles were shaken out to dry, then raked back. Eventually they were heaped into a pike and carted back to be stacked close to the farmhouse. A sweep yielded eight or nine kyles, with two sweeps-worth, one either side, making up a pike. All very mysterious and shrouded in tradition.

Apart from John, who was still at school, the work would have been shared out among his mother and father, a hind from the tied cottage, a servant-girl from the house and an aunt's maid from Harlow Field. Then a hayman would be hired, probably from the same Irish family as in previous years and decades.

Baling came to Sillywrea in the early 1960s and did away with many of the worries about finding labour. Today horse-drawn machines still cut, turn and rake, because John loves his horses, but a tractor is hired to pull an International square-baler, bought at a sale a few years ago. There is no temptation to take on bank loans for capital machinery.

Swath-turning is light work, for a single horse. The machine is simple and effective, essentially an axle between two circular discs which turn in a clockwise direction and carry steel prongs to toss the hay. It was easy work the summer I was involved, but dusty and hot, and the flies sometimes troubled the younger horses sharing evening duties.

Before baling the hay was turned again, but this time with a machine that tossed the swaths into a single row, 'two rows up,' to make it quicker to gather. The baler soon finished the Barley Riggs, after which David took round the horse-rake to clean up.

'If hay's worth gathering it's worth leading,' said John, implying that once it is into bales it should be taken in as quickly as possible. Bales can be stooked in the field in such a way that most rain runs off, but

not without some risk of spontaneous combustion. Sillywrea is famous for its heavy bales: heavy to load and heavy to stack. A hundred bales to the acre is an average yield; farms using artificial fertiliser would expect about 140. The Barley Riggs, on the rise towards Moss Flats, would bring in 1200 bales.

Three extra men were called in to help with the leading; all 'worked loose.' Leading started in the late afternoon to give the team time to assemble, and then it was a three- or four-hour job to clear what had been made ready. The farm buildings needed to take in over 4000 bales altogether, sufficient for six months of winter feed. Sillywrea has never had to buy in bales and in some years there are hundreds to spare. These are kept as insurance, just in case...

Some of the barns around the yard were already full before the bales from the Barley Riggs came down. One after another, cattle byres were stacked to the rafters. The cattle would have to 'eat their way out,' so their quarters would be empty by the time they were driven in for the winter. Nobody spoke as the work went on. Four horse-drawn bogies (low, sideless carts) were used, so that at any time there would be one loading, one leading and one going out. The work seemed relentless – at least to me: by now my back was aching and my hands were raw from heaving against the twine.

Eric had the key job of stacking, moving among the cobwebbed rafters as the bales reached higher and higher to fill the eaves. Soon there was no more space and the next bogey was sent to another outbuilding, this time a hemmel or stone sheep-shed. Swallows were feeding fledglings inside, hovering for a second at the doorway before weaving past the working men. More bales arrived; each bogey carried about 25 and there was always another load close behind. Then there was a lull as John counted what was left and came back to say it was nearly in. Eric leaned back against the hay and sucked a green straw, then spoke about his old white van and the tree planting he had been doing at Falstone, a day's drive into the forest.

A sickly-sweet smell of new hay filled the air. One by one cockchafer beetles launched themselves from the loose hay and buzzed out into the fading light.

Dennis Hedley making silage with an old John Deere baler at Hexham. All was going well until one of the belts broke.

David Wise turning hay in late June, Sillywrea Farm near Langley in south Northumberland.

Swath-turner at the side of the Quarry Field, Sillywrea Farm.

The last hay bale being fitted into the loft of an outbuilding, Sillywrea Farm.

Alan Bousfield of Greenhills, Harwood-in-Teesdale, cutting hay at Collinson's. This land is owned by the Raby estate, so all the barns are whitewashed. If the weather is good the grass is cut and 'bobbed' or turned twice, then gathered into a row and left for another hour or two before baling.

Above: *Baling hay at Earnwell Farm, Ireshopeburn in Weardale, County Durham.*

A square hay bale lying in the field at Earnwell Farm. It looks heavy.

Above: *Christine English with a team of helpers loading hay bales at Earnwell Farm, Ireshopeburn in Weardale.*

Stacking hay into the barn at Bowlees, Teesdale.

Shepherd Peter Dixon, of Stobbs in Redesdale, filing a rams-horn; the start of months of work to create a prize-winning crook for a stick-dressing competition.

TWELVE

Back End Sales and Shows

My notebook contains one brief entry for 24 February 2001: 'Should have been in Cheviots but Foot and Mouth at Heddon. Waiting to see if any other outbreaks locally.' A week later, on 2 March, I wrote: 'Snow lying all week. F+M getting a grip. The countryside closing down.' It got worse over the following months, of course. It affected my work, but not badly. For me it was an irritation, because I could not go for a walk or finish a few photo-shoots. But for some it was a catastrophe: the last straw.

Living independent or lonely lives, talking to dogs and resorting to conversations with gateposts, people in the hills need to get out – to go shopping, watch a football match, take their children to ballet classes – just to reassure themselves they are still human. Being quarantined, exiled, excluded from society, was one of the worst effects of the 2001 Nemesis. Every get-together was cancelled, which served to emphasise how important marts and shepherds' shows had been in bringing people together. In the desolation of empty fields, there was nothing to look forward to.

Some of the smaller stock markets have not reopened after Foot and Mouth. Farmers who would have sent their sheep and sucklers to Bellingham or Rothbury now send them to the new mart at Hexham instead. There is less business to do on market day too, because farmers often sell stock over the phone or by internet. But to establish a guide price and have your stock properly valued there is no substitute for working it through a mart.

After having photographed at several hill farms in the early 1990s I made a point of following lambs and tups from their home hills through the sale ring. I still have schedules from Bellingham Mart for 18 September 1993, listing 12,000 mule ewe lambs for sale that day, and another from 21 October 1995 of 15,000 breeding ewes and store lambs. Typical sales, not big but respectable. Many of the farms I knew in Northumberland were represented in the schedule listings: Brieredge, Langleeford, Bellshiel and Barrowburn. Names that sound as if they belong in a different time: The Raw, Shittleheugh, Grasslees and Smiddywell Rigg. When I went to the great tup sales at Kelso I recognised many of the same names in the sale details and the same faces in the crowd; the circle is small.

I have never seen anybody smile at a mart or give themselves away by getting excited. There is a gloss of gloom over the proceedings. Everyone knows that the auction price can never be good enough, whether buying or selling. Conversations are undertaken at length but with as few words as possible. Long silences are punctuated by a sharp intake of breath or a shake of the head.

When I asked someone about this I was told 'bad trade means long faces.' And trade was usually bad. Perhaps over the decades farmers have grown used to expecting the worst and are just waiting for it to happen. Which it did in the mid-1990s when the prices crashed. I was at one of the first autumn marts when the expected disaster in the sale ring became apparent, but you could not read it on anyone's face. Since then things have got better and worse, and now a little bit better again. Perhaps it is a good idea not to be too demonstrative.

Putting on a Show

Spring and back-end shows are a summer treat for everyone, an unholy mix of livestock judging, family sports and fluke-drench demonstrations. Again, there is a serious business behind the social imperative. Farmers spend weeks preparing their animals, crimping and shampooing fleeces, dusting talc on the Cheviots and oiling the faces of Blackface and Swaledales. A few rosettes enhance a farm's reputation and the value of its produce; for once it is commonplace to see farmers smiling as they allow themselves to be photographed with prize animals. Local newspapers carry full-page spreads under headlines like 'Pigs hog the limelight at the Friendly Show.'

At a time when less than two per cent of the population works in agriculture, visitor numbers at rural shows increase steadily year by year. Some competitions at local shows, like pony-classes and small-pipes, have grown in popularity whilst others, like vegetable-growing, have diminished. This suggests that it is incomers who are the life-blood of the shows but this is not really the case – the organisers are usually computer-literate farming families and the shows would continue even if only local people attended.

Among the traditional skills stick-dressing still thrives and has a cult following among shepherds of a certain age. Quoits and Cumberland wrestling help to sustain the exotic and esoteric character of events. Most people who go to the annual shows hardly glance at the sheep or cattle pens. But in 2002 when there were no animal classes – a residual effect of Foot and Mouth – everything seemed diminished and trivial. As in the wider countryside, agriculture is the key to the culture.

Some of the spring shows are the most enjoyable, because they are small and concentrate on local matters like sheep: Tan Hill, High Force and the Roman Wall shows are all a delight if the weather is kind. The back-end shows like Wolsingham and Glendale are fun too and they attract good crowds. Last but not least is Alwinton Show, the latest of the Northumberland shepherds' shows, always held in October even though it is a remote place and it always seems to be disrupted by rain, hail and snow.

Blackboard with the day's total, Bellingham Mart.

Sarah Smith-Jackson with her Bluefaced Leicester, best junior exhibit at the Roman Wall Show.

Glendale showground, at the foot of the Cheviots, near Wooler in Northumberland.

Bobbie Scott judging Cheviots at Glendale Show. Local farmers and shepherds look on: Ambrose Anderson, John Guiry, Michael Elliot, Richard Dixon, Craig Weir and John Elliot.

Willie Twizell showing off a Blackface ewe, Glendale Show near Wooler.

Charlie Armstrong judging Blackface gimmers in the pens at Glendale Show.

Taking the strain for the tug-of-war, Ingram Show in the Breamish Valley. Fawdon West Hill and Ewe Hill in the distance.

Cumberland wrestling, Roman Wall Show. The showground is at Steel Rigg: in the far distance two walkers are heading east along Hadrian's Wall.

Dick and Greg Dalton of Wellhope Farm in Weardale getting a Swaledale tup ready for the sale at St John's Chapel: 'For a tup the main features to look for are the hair on the forehead being black and wiry, the muzzle big and white: the legs long and spotted on the front, with a clear edge between black and white. It should have a good square shape, like table-legs at the corners. A judge should be able to skim his trilby through the front legs.' Dick is applying the final touch – a light brush of peat to the fleece, which makes the white of the muzzle and legs stand out.

Brisk business in the mart ring: the autumn lamb sales at Bellingham Mart, Northumberland.

All eyes on the auctioneer, Bellingham Mart, Northumberland.

Walter Brown of Ilderton Moor with his nephew, also Walter Brown, of Langleeford, studying the schedule and comparing prices at Bellingham Mart.

A quiet word on the back row: Bellingham Mart.

Looking over the pens: the annual tup sale at St John's Chapel, Weardale.

Studying the schedule in a quiet moment away from the sale ring. Annual tup sale,
St John's Chapel.

Welcome hay on a cold December morning. Michael Jameson among his cattle, West Hotbank Farm near Bardon Mill.

THIRTEEN

Sucklers

Farmers are more influenced by fashion than they would care to admit. Crops come and go, breeds appear and thrive for a few decades. Cattle in particular have suffered from market trends and local prejudices. Breeds that were county-show champions for one generation can be relegated to the rare breeds tent for the next.

There was a time when the moors of Durham and Northumberland were stocked with cattle rather than sheep. A couple of centuries ago anyone walking the foothills would have seen wintering herds of 'Irish' store cattle. These were bought in to fatten and sell at local marts; their pedigree was dubious.

Not so the herds of Galloways that were established at about this time – they represented the cutting edge of agricultural innovation. Galloways were bred for the hills and they were robust and suited to the climate. Unfortunately, they were also small and slow-growing, so their popularity has been relatively brief. For a while in the early 1990s it looked as though they might make a comeback because of a renewed interest in premium quality beef, but BSE restrictions – the imposition of a thirty-month rule – dealt the breed another blow.

Galloways can still be seen on a few farms, notably in the Wall Country where the Whin Sill makes an appropriate backdrop for chunky black cattle. Traditionally, they were put to a beef Shorthorn bull to produce a blue-grey calf, which was sold on for fattening and breeding.

Galloways are pretty and they make very good mothers, but they can be very aggressive. When their calves are taken away from them they become homicidal – I discovered hidden abilities as a rock-climber when charged by an aggrieved Galloway at the foot of Peel Crags. She stood baying at me for an hour before letting me down from the cliff face.

Big Breeds in the Big Country

In valleys and lowlands the length and breadth of Northumbria dual-purpose shorthorns were the core of most farm herds until butter-making finished in the 1950s. With the establishment of suckler herds many cattlemen experimented with Hereford x Friesians, but eventually the Hereford bulls became too short and 'gutty' and the Friesians were getting too much Holstein blood in their veins.

So farmers took to the Continentals and it has been that way ever since. This change could not have happened had it not been for the new system of in-wintered cattle. Instead of being left on the pastures, surviving on 'tath' or foggaged (dried up) grass, cattle were tethered in old byres, stables and cart sheds and fed hay, straw and chopped swede. The land-scape has benefited over the last few years by not being overgrazed or poached, but farmers have now built big stock sheds with rows of bagged silage outside – not everyone's idea of an idyllic rural scene.

David Wise trimming hair from the face of a suckler cow, indoors for the winter at Sillywrea Farm.

The Continental breeds – Charolais, Limousin, Simmental, Blonde d'Aquitaine – are giants compared with the traditional British breeds, but they are wimps when it comes to the weather. In-wintering has solved the problem. Fast-growing and with good 'conformation', they have dominated meat markets for the past twenty years.

At first it seemed that the Charolais was going to be the most popular breed – it is certainly the most handsome. But part of its good looks, as demonstrated in the picture I took at Thrunton, is that it is big-boned. Any cross -bred offspring killed out at 600 kilos might be half bone and waste – a third more than for other Continentals. These days 70 per cent of the national suckler herd is Limousin; i.e. a Limousin bull crossed with a Limousin x Friesian cow. The result is a sameness about farmyards and a sameness in the quality of meat available in supermarkets.

When you walk in the uplands in winter now you rarely see any cattle. For up to six or seven months they are in the sheds. They are sometimes mated there and many give birth there. At Sillywrea Farm, which is on the 600ft contour, they bring in their cattle a little later, towards Christmas.

I was in the yard at Easter one year when they let them out again. David Wise told me to keep well clear because they would be excited. In fact they went potty, dancing and leaping like springbok and galloping up towards the Thackey Field like wildebeest. When I have seen cattle in the vastness of the Cheviots or Lunedale it seems to me that they take on the grace of their ancestors and become a natural part of the landscape.

Galloway cow and blue-grey calf: Sewingshields Farm on Hadrian's Wall, South Northumberland.

Hay for the Galloways: Angus Murray of Sewingshields Farm, in the pastures north of the Wall.

From a distance Galloway cattle look big and black. Close-up they look small and rusty.
Angus Murray of Sewingshields Farm, somewhere in the emptiness of Haughton Common.

Ian Campbell of Thrunton Farm, near Glanton in Northumberland, with a prize-winning Charolais bull, 'Thrunton Invincible'.

Hexham Morris dancing to Lads a'Bunchum: The Flags, outside Hexham Abbey.

FOURTEEN

Kirn Supper

In the arable lands of Durham and Cleveland a rough 'kirn dolly' was made from the last sheaf of corn scythed for the harvest, with the words:

Weel bun and better shorn
Is Maister Morley's corn;
We hev her, we hev her,
As fast as a feather.
Hip, hip, hooray!

...and then everybody trooped into the farm-house to get tipsy at a special Kirn or Mell Supper. Whether it was as idyllic as it sounds, I doubt. But I like to think it was a key moment in the farming year when working men and women were able to celebrate the seasons and enjoy themselves at the farmer's expense.

In the Bronze Age, cereal crops were grown in the uplands wherever the ground was suitable: the climate was a degree or two warmer then which made all the difference. Nobody has been able to grow cereals above the thousand foot mark since. For several hundred years until the 1950s, the grain crop of the foothills was oats; now it is barley. Waving fields of grain 'ripe unto harvest' are a wonderful sight, particularly in the attractive landscape of the Durham Plain and in the Cheviot foothills.

Whether there has always been a harvest celebration I am not sure, but several old labourers in the Cheviots remember kirn feasts at the larger estates like Lilburn and Ford. More recently, harvest suppers have been a feature of village halls, keeping the communities together, though over the last couple of years I have noticed these have evolved into Harvest Discos.

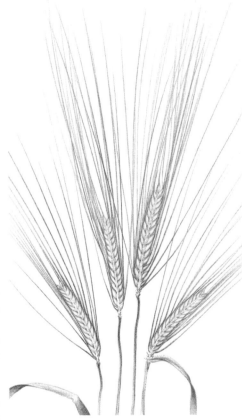

Further south in England, the wheat harvest was celebrated in the same way. In Central France in August 1995 we spent an afternoon at a 'Fête des Battages' in the little town of St Alvère: the locals had built an old-fashioned barley rick and were busy most of the day threshing the sheaves with a steam-driven threshing machine and a binder. Afterwards a young girl brought a handful of grain around so that everyone could share symbolically in the harvest. Then, of course, the evening descended into a open-air party with a lot of cheese and wine and accordion music.

You only had to look at the numbers of people involved in the threshing to realise why agriculture has had to move on. But it looked and sounded wonderful. I imagine the corresponding Kirn Supper of Northumbria would have been similar, but held in a barn and with beer rather than wine to get the dancing started.

John Barleycorn

Dancing has always been a part of country life. It still surprises me to see sane and sensible people losing it on the dance floor. Ritual dancing – not line-dancing but longsword or morris – fascinates me: nobody really understands what it is about but it has echoes of antiquity about it: crude, threatening and obscure. Deeply out of fashion for most of the last two hundred years it has survived, perverse and subversive as punk. It made me proud to see our sons Andrew and Neal dance in the Hexham Morris – it was something I knew I could never master myself and I was impressed that they were able to ignore the sneers of their friends, at least for a while.

I had thought that morris, a rural tradition unlike longsword, was not danced much in Northumbria, but I now wonder if it simply died out unnoticed until the '70s revival. Recently I picked up a mildewed 1950s guide to 'country dancing' in a second-hand bookshop and discovered a photograph in it of Cecil Sharpe and George Butterworth noting down tunes from a dance team at Beadnell in the 1900s.

I wonder if anyone living at Beadnell now can believe that the local farm labourers and fishermen once performed such strange rites, or that serious composers paid attention to them? The idea that people originally danced to celebrate the coming of spring or the harvest had clearly been lost on the Beadnell team – like every authentic old picture I have seen of morris dancing, nobody is smiling. Perhaps it was a glum affair, performed out of duty or for a shilling from the local squire.

John Barleycorn, another manifestation of the Kirn god, grows a beard and is cut down in late summer. A percentage of the barley crop still goes for malting in the North East but most is kept to feed cattle.

People experiment with other fodder grains such as triticale – a wheat x rye hybrid – but barley is king.

Combine harvesters are fearsome machines, when they work. It takes two men half a day to harvest a 20-acre field – one to drive the combine and one to ferry the grain back to the farm in a tractor. A combine driver, freelance or working loose, will earn about £5 an hour. Not a lucrative or easy job, particularly if the combine is temperamental and has to be adjusted every few minutes.

Following a combine as it works into a field is a noisy and dusty experience: a beautiful golden quilt is transformed by a flurry of flying blades into processed grain and straw bales, leaving behind a wasteland with a stitchwork of dry stubble. Eventually, as the square of standing corn shrinks in the middle, there is the excitement of seeing hares and foxes making a dash for freedom.

Triticale (rye x wheat) ready for harvest.

'Two weeks late and still a bit moist': Jonathan Beniams testing the softness of the grains to see if the crop is ready. Thorngrafton, near Newbrough (pronounced 'Newbruff') in south Northumberland.

Jonathan Beniams combining a 30-acre field of triticale – the grain is being transferred to a tractor and trailer to be taken back to Michael Gibson's farm at Newbrough.

Late-September afternoon: Jonathan Beniams and an old combine harvester, Thorngrafton, Newbrough in South Northumberland.

Loading straw bales, near Wallington in Northumberland.

Stubble and straw: Thorngrafton, Newbrough.

FIFTEEN

Deep Midwinter

Earth often stands hard as iron for weeks at a time on Cross Fell or in the high Cheviots. It can snow in June, though the 'back end' in September/October is usually soft and clear and is many people's favourite time of year.

On the hill farms November marks the start of winter, and it is surprising how often there is a heavy fall of snow in the first week. On many farms this coincides with an important time for the sheep as the tups are driven out onto the high ground to mate with the hill ewes.

I followed Jim Wilson of Ingram Farm one morning as he tried to bully a gang of Blackface tups up onto Turf Knowe. They were not enthusiastic about having to go. Snow had been falling lightly for an hour but then a piercing wind gusted from the north-west and we were soon bracing ourselves against a blizzard. The tups became bolshie and stood their ground against the collies, but eventually they had no option but to continue through the drifts. It took another hour to get them onto the appropriate cut of the hill, where the ewes were already settled in for the worst of the weather.

Each tup serves about a hundred ewes over a three week period. By early December the die would be cast and next spring's lambs would be on the way. The tups by then would have earned a rest. We left them somewhere near South Planting; in fact the visibility was so poor I had no idea where we were and relied on Jim's collies to lead me down to the road at Bulby's Wood. Fortunately, the snow on the road was only a couple of inches deep and there was no ice underneath. I would be able to drive out of the valley if I went straight away without stopping at the farm for a cup of tea.

The next day all the snow had gone and the valley farms were clear. Not so the high hills, Cushat Law, Hedgehope and Cheviot, which were all white for another week. It was the middle of the month before I managed to visit Bleakhope where Stuart Nelson was getting his Swaledales ready. Bleakhope is the most remote farm in the Cheviots. More significantly it has no inbye land or working fields close to the farmhouse. This is a big problem at tupping time. A sheep farm relies on new blood; a percentage of the ewes is replaced each year by the best of the new crop of young female sheep. These are known as hoggs. In their first winter the hoggs are not robust enough to carry a lamb, which means that on most farms they are either kept separate from the tups or are transported down the valley to hired pasture.

At Bleakhope neither of these options is possible, so they 'breek' the hoggs – i.e. they sew a patch of hessian onto the backside of each young sheep to keep out the tup. It sounds primitive, but it works. Stuart Nelson was surprisingly deft with a darning needle on a cold November morning, first folding the hessian squares at the edges and scoring them by rubbing them against a fence-post, then stitching the patch into place over the sheep's tail. The last thread of string was tied to the tail, so that the breek patch lifted just enough to let the sheep defecate. Ingenious and simple. Only two or three farms in the Cheviots still go through the time-consuming business of breeking their hoggs. I have seen it being done in the Lake District where it is called 'clouting t'winters', though the farmer I photographed there used patches of orange blanket which looked very odd on his grey Herdwicks.

After the morning at Bleakhope I walked up the ancient Salters Road with Stuart's brother Graham, onto the top of Shill Moor for the great sweep of a view across to Cheviot. The wind was so cold that my eyes streamed and my fingers were too numb to feel the camera's shutter-release: we retreated to the farm for whisky and walnut cake and I was on my way home before the wet track froze.

The hardest weather in the hills usually arrives after Christmas. February is the worst month and March the most capricious. The best a shepherd can do on short winter days is check his or her stock and keep them alive. Hill sheep are good at finding their own food but deep snow makes life difficult. Haying is then a mission of mercy and I have been out on several occasions with shepherds and farmers to 'look the sheep' and to spread a bale of hay on the frozen ground. It never looks enough to keep the animals alive but it sees them by. On the first day or two of a cold snap sheep can't be bothered much with hay and they have to be whistled in, but they get hungrier with each long night and eventually there is a scrum of flying hoofs every time the shepherd appears. Whistling then becomes a way of imposing calm authority amid chaos.

The Tar Barrels

I have often heard farm labourers whistling as they work, but the only time I have heard anyone singing in the fields was on a March morning near Butterknowle in County Durham when I had stopped for lunch in the half-shelter of a hedge and was suddenly assaulted by a full-blooded rendition of 'Voulez-Vous'. Hidden over a tussock ridge was a girl in a blue boiler suit digging a pit to bury a dead sheep. I was impressed, more by the vehemence of the spadework than by her singing. It occurred to me that the working countryside is not a place for music, whether it be the 'distant voice across the meadow' of Vaughan William's 'Pastoral' Symphony, or an old Abba classic.

Farmers are disinclined to sing traditional labouring songs. On the other hand, they do seem to enjoy country music – i.e. American poor-white rural music, diluted to taste. There is a paradox about this that has something to do with being English; we have given away our own roots music and are now buying it back to play through headphones in tractor cabs. What is most disturbing is that the country music people listen to is not the edgy stuff of Steve Earle but the tacky doggerel of Slim Whitman. This is a test of tolerance that I fail every time.

On New Year's Eve the King's Head at Allendale puts on a special supper and for several years we went to it before the midnight procession of the Tar Barrels. Imagine a scene of utter pagan chaos and that is the Tar Barrels. After sitting in the warm with a pint of Theakstons, the custom is to stagger out into the cold dark night and gather in a crowd to watch a group of cross-dressed 'guisers' parade with burning half-barrels on their heads.

I have stood on the streets of Castleton in the Peak District on Garland Day and listened in reverence as a band marched up and down playing 'Pudding in a Basket' over and over again. But at Allendale the band plays 'Daisy, Daisy' and 'She'll be Coming Round the Mountain'. Not mysterious music in keeping with the ritual of the barrels but fun music to jig along to as you wait for the bonfire.

And so to the end of another notebook:

Downstairs from the long room 11.30. Stairway choked with people, sitting in pairs, close. Clown and leopard man. Sound of an accordion and 'Rolling Home' from the back room. Outside, crowd expectant. Bitter-cold night. Rucks and ridges of ice on the cobbles. Snow on the roofs and on top of the pile of brashings. Bright Sirius in the south sky. Stood for ten minutes. Everyone waiting. Glow of fire from beside the church/hidden by the crowd. Then a cheer as the fire-brands come into view and barrels are lit and the procession

forms up. Led by silver band playing Blaydon Races. Slow double row of colourful guisers washed now with gold flickering light. Steady, all balancing the half-barrels on their heads and keeping pace. Crowd pressing from every side, only a foot or two from the burning barrels; children weaving among parents, some running with the column. From the far side of the village, the glow on the terrace of buildings. Around the square and back. Band still playing jaunty tunes. Barrels thrown down around the foot of the bonfire, one at a time, ringing it in fire. Figures dance and flicker. Soon the whole bonfire is up – curtains of flame and thousands of sparks, rising up with grey smoke and taken by the swirl of wind. Everyone now shouting. Midnight: The old year in flames. People pushing through the crowd to be with friends, lost in the excitement. 'Auld Lang Syne'. Then a silence as the people look to each other and wish each other a new year, or warm themselves and wait for the church bells to peel. Bonfire orange on indigo. Back to the King's Head through a smoky crush, and upstairs for hot soup. To the car and back in a slow procession along the snowy road to Hexham.

Once the bonfire has died there is nothing left to do at Allendale and people soon disperse into the pubs or back home. This last time we went to the Tar Barrels we arrived home at one o'clock in time for an impromptu family sing-along to a fiddle and guitar, with a glass of whisky and a sit around the embers of a peat fire. As I climbed the stairs afterwards, probably humming 'Blaydon Races', I could see the shelf where a big pile of photographs was accumulating to be made into a book, somewhere ages and ages hence.

A shaft of winter sunlight in the shed at Low Bleakhope (pronounced 'Blake-up') in the Cheviots. Stuart and Edwin Nelson sorting sheep. The pheasants hanging on the line – out of reach of the dogs – are for a game pie.

Stuart Nelson 'breeking' a Swaledale hogg at Low Bleakhope Farm. The unmated young sheep has a patch of hessian stitched over its backside to stop a tup from mating with it. Hoggs are not robust enough to carry a lamb in their first spring, and there is no 'inbye' ground available where they can be kept separate.

Michael Jameson haying sheep at West Hotbank, north of Hadrian's Wall near Bardon Mill. Late December: two or three of the sheep are snow-blind and others have been pawing the ground to uncover grass. After a week of snow it has been minus 12° C overnight. No sign of a let-up.

Jim Wilson driving out tups in a November blizzard: Ingram Farm in the Cheviots.

Allendale Tar Barrels, New Year's Eve. The procession makes its way through the town, burning barrels balanced on heads and the band playing 'Blaydon Races'.

A tricky moment as the burning tar barrels are emptied at the base of the bonfire. The 'guisers' are dressed in bizarre costumes – Harlequins, sailors, clowns – scary in the flickering firelight.

Flames and sparks swirl as the bonfire lights up the square at Allendale. The clock chimes the New Year in, everyone sings 'Auld Lang Syne': the world moves on.